The World's
Easiest Guide
to
Using the APA

A User-Friendly Manual for
Formatting Research Papers
According to the
American Psychological Association
Style Guide

3rd Edition

Carol J. Amato

STARGAZER
Publishing Company
Corona, California

D1288534

Published by Stargazer Publishing Company
PO Box 77002
Corona, CA 92877-0100
(800) 606-7895
(951) 898-4619
FAX (951) 898-4633
Corporate e-mail: stargazer@stargazerpub.com
Order e-mail: orders@stargazerpub.com
website: http://www.stargazerpub.com

All material in this book corresponds to the Fifth Edition of the *Publication Manual of the American Psychological Association*. This book is intended for undergraduate use only.

First printing, 1995
Second printing, 1995
Third printing, 1996
Fourth printing, 1998, revised
Fifth printing, 1999
Sixth printing, 2000
Seventh printing, 2002, revised
Eighth printing, 2003
Ningth printing, 2004

ISBN: 0-9713756-6-6 (College Edition, paper, spiral bound)
0-9713756-7-4 (Library Edition, paper, perfect bound)

Library of Congress Catalog Card Number: 2002101990

Publisher's Cataloging-in-Publication
(Provided by Quality Books, Inc.)

Amato, Carol J.
    The world's easiest guide to using the APA : a user-friendly manual for formatting research papers according to the American Psychological Association style guide / Carol J. Amato. -- 3rd ed.
    p. cm.
    Includes bibliographical references.
    LCCN 2002101990
    ISBN 0-9713756-6-6 (spiral)
    ISBN 0-9713756-7-4 (perfect)

    1. Psychology—Authorship—Handbooks, manuals, etc.
2. Psychological literature—Publishing—Handbooks, manuals, etc. I. Title.

BF76.7.A468 2002   808'.06615
                          QBI02-200430

Table of Contents

Chapter 7 Creating a List of References, Cont'd

Chapter 7 *Creating a List of References*, Cont'd.

Chapter 7 Creating a List of References, *Cont'd.*

List of Figures

List of Figures, Cont'd.

List of Figures, Cont'd.

List of Figures, Cont'd.

List of Figures, Cont'd.

List of Figures, Cont'd.

List of Tables

Introduction

The World's Easiest Guide to Using the APA, 3rd Edition, gives undergraduate students a simple, clear-cut explanation of how to use the 5th edition of the American Psychological Association (APA) style guide to format their reports. This book is also designed as a guide for faculty who are teaching students this particular style.

What is a style guide?

Most departments in colleges and universities require that students' papers be presented in the same manner. They each have a specific way sources must be documented. The books that supply these directions are called style guides. A style guide not only shows how to document sources, however, but also explains the rules for creating many other parts of the document, such as:

- which font (typestyle) to use

- how to create and place headers and/or footers

- the number of lines per page (i.e., whether you should single- or double-space the document)

- whether to use upper- or lower-case on certain words, titles, names, etc.

- how to space out such items as mathematical symbols or equations and scientific formulas

- how to cite paraphrased material and direct quotations and how to reference sources

- whether the document should be printed single-sided or double-sided

- how to place figures and tables

There are many style guides. Besides the APA, the ones commonly used in colleges and universities are:

- MLA (Modern Language Association)

- Chicago (The University of Chicago's *Manual of Style*)

The disciplines that commonly use APA besides psychology, of course, are nursing, education, business, criminology, and environmental science.

If you took an introductory psychology or communications course, you might have been introduced to the APA through such sources as *A Writer's Reference*, the *Little, Brown Compact Handbook*, and/or the *Publication Manual* put out by the APA itself.

Why aren't these sources enough?

A Writer's Reference and the *Little, Brown Compact Handbook* contain only a few pages of explanation. The *APA Publication Manual* does explain everything, but it is really meant for professional psychologists submitting articles to the American Psychological Association's own journal; therefore, some of the guidelines are very confusing and/or do not apply to formatting reports at the undergraduate level. Writing a report or project is formidable enough without having to tackle the complexities of the APA's *Publication Manual*.

The World's Easiest Guide to Using the APA takes you step-by-step through the creation of your entire research paper, including detailed instructions on how to format your citations and references.

I hope that *The World's Easiest Guide to Using the APA* proves to be just that for you.

Chapter 1

Setting Up Your Pages

A report includes the following:

- Title page

- Executive Summary (optional)

- Table of Contents

- List of Figures (if more than five)

- List of Tables (if more than five)

- Body of document

- References

- Appendix(ces) (optional)

This chapter talks about creating the body pages of a document. It includes specific instructions on the following:

- Using the correct font

- Page layout

    - Setting the margins
    - Formatting the header
    - Formatting the headings
    - Creating body text
    - Formatting the page numbers

Using the Correct Font

With the availability of desktop-publishing programs today, it's easy to feel that one should create fancy covers and use various fonts to make a document look good. As nice as this might appear, you must use *manuscript* style; that is, double-spacing with roughly 25 lines per page. That means just plain type, folks, just plain type.

Use one of the following fonts in 12-point size:

- Courier

- Courier New

- Times

- Times Roman

- Times New Roman

Figure 1 shows examples of these fonts. As you can see, Courier and Courier New may appear exactly the same; likewise, Times Roman and Times New Roman. The name will depend on the software you are using; for example, if you are using MS Word 97 or above, you will find these fonts listed as Courier New and Times New Roman.

```
This is Courier

This is Courier New
```
This is Times

This is Times Roman

This is Times New Roman

Figure 1. Examples of Acceptable Fonts.

Page Layout

Your document's pages will consist of the following elements:

- Margins

- Header

- Headings

- Body text

- Graphics

This section explains how to create the margins, header, headings, and body text. Detailed information on how to place graphics is explained in Chapter 2.

Setting the Margins

Set the margins of your document to the following:

- Left margin = 1"

- Top margin = 1"

- Right margin = 1"

- Bottom margin = 1"

Refer to Figure 2.

EXCEPTION: *If you intend to bind your document, you may set the left margin to 1½".*

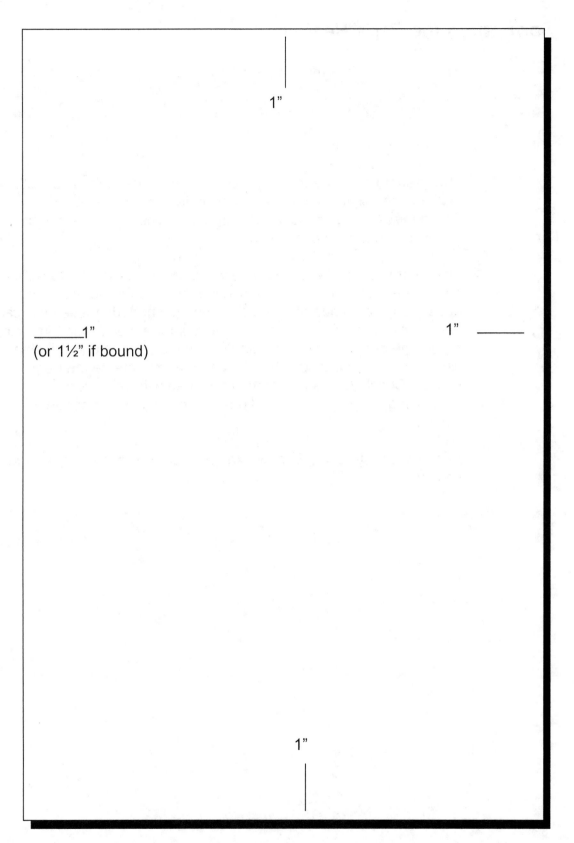

Figure 2. Correct Margin Settings.

Formatting the Page Header

Each of your pages must have a header consisting of the following:

- Short version of the title

- Page number

The header should be the first two or three words of the title. Let's say that the full title of your report or project is "Problems with Reorganization Factors at ABC Company." The short title can be "Problems With Reorganization."

The short title and the page number are on the same line; leave five spaces between the two, as shown in Figure 3. This format must appear on every page of your document. Do not add these physically to each page, or when you add or move information around in your report, the headers could end up in the middle of the page. Instead, use your word processor's header command to create the page header. Check the documentation provided with your word-processing program for instructions on how to use the header command.

Appendices A through E show examples of full reports with a page header.

Problems With Reorganization   3

Lorem ipsum dolor sit amet, consectetuer adipisci elit, sed diam nonummy nibh eusmod tin cidunt ut loreet dolore magna aliquam erat volutpat. Ut wisi ad minim veniam, quis nostrud exerci tation ulcorper suscipit lobortis nisl ut aliquip ex ea commodo consequat.

Duis atem vel eum iriure dolor in hendrerit in putate velit esse molestie consequat, vel illum dolore feugiat nulla facilisis at vero eros et accumsan et odio dignissim qui blandit praesent luptatum zzril del augue duis dolore te feugait nulla facilisi.

Nam liber tempor cum soluta nobis eleifend id congue nihil imperdiet doming id quod mazim placerat possim assum. Lorem ipsum dolor sit amet, consectetuer adipisci elit, sed diam nonummy nibh eusmod tin cidunt ut loreet dolore magna aliquam erat volutpat.

Ut wisi ad minim veniam, quis nostrud exertione ulcorper suscipit lobortis nisl ut aliquip ex commodo consequat. Duis atem vel eum iriure dolor in hendrerit putate velit esse molestie consequat, vel illum dolore feugiat nulla facilisis at vero eros et accumsan ad

Figure 3. Example Header.

Formatting the Headings

Determining the Number of Levels

Headings (as opposed to head-*ers*) are the section titles in your document. For instance, a report might have the following headings:

- Report Title

- Body Heading(s) (example: "Findings")

- Conclusion

- References

This setup uses one heading level; however, if the body were further subdivided into subheadings, two heading levels would exist (i.e., dividing "Findings" into "Attitudes Among Management Personnel" and "Attitudes Among Employees").

Every heading level must contain at least two listings; otherwise, incorporate the material into the heading above that level. In other words, you cannot have just one subheading under "Findings"; you must have at least two.

Figure 4 shows an example of the headings for a report. As you can see, this report uses three levels of headings; that is, it divides the information into three levels of importance:

- Title of the article   (1st level heading)

- Main heading level   (1st level heading)

- Subheading level   (2nd level heading)

- Subsubheading level   (3rd level heading)

Let's say you are using the format shown in Figure 4. You may decide to further subdivide the headings "Company-owned" and "Employee-owned" into brand names. If so, you have now reached four levels of headings (see page 20.) Some very long reports may include a fifth level heading (see page 22).

Count the number of heading levels in the section of your report with the most breakdowns. You must select the heading styles based on this number (see page 12).

```
        Pros and Cons of Electronic Communication
           At Three Large Companies (Level 1)


  Types of Electronic Communication at Company A (Level 1)*
     E-mail (Level 2)
     Pagers (Level 2)
     Cell Phones (Level 2)
        Company-owned (Level 3)
        Employee-owned (Level 3)
     Fax Machines (Level 2)


  Types of Electronic Communication at Company B (Level 1)
     E-mail (Level 2)
     Pagers (Level 2)
     Cell Phones (Level 2)
     Fax Machines (Level 2)


  Types of Electronic Communication at Company C (Level 1)
     E-mail (Level 2)
     Pagers (Level 2)
     Cell Phones (Level 2)
     Fax Machines (Level 2)


Conclusion (Level 1)
```

Figure 4. Levels of Headings Used in a Report With Three Levels of Headings.

*The APA style does not use the word "Introduction" before the introduction because the title of the report is at the top of the page (unless a title page is used; in that event, the first paragraph of the introduction begins at the top with no heading). The headings shown above appear in the report after the introduction.

Selecting the Heading Styles

The APA requires you to use different heading *styles* depending on the number of heading *levels* you have. While the APA *Publication Manual* itself refers to these styles as "levels," they are called "styles" in this book to avoid confusion with the levels of importance you are using in your report. *The World's Easiest Guide* does follow the APA numbering system for these styles, however.

The APA has five heading styles, as shown in Figure 5. In this figure, "flush left" refers to flush with the *margin*—not with the edge of the paper. This section shows the styles to use for the different numbers of heading levels. Most short reports use one or two heading levels; more comprehensive reports may use three or more.

As mentioned on page 10, to determine which styles to use, count the number of heading levels in your report that contains the most heading levels and turn to the instructions in this book for that number of headings:

1 heading level   page 14

2 heading levels   page 16

3 heading levels   page 18

4 heading levels   page 20

5 heading levels   page 22

Use the selected set of headings throughout your document. Pay close attention to the upper/lower case requirements.

CENTERED, UPPERCASE HEADING   (Style 5)

Centered, Initial Caps Heading   (Style 1)

Centered, Italicized, Initial Caps Heading, (Style 2)

Double-spaced and Centered When Going to a

Succeeding Line

Flush Left, Italicized, Initial Caps Heading, and   (Style 3)
Single-spaced When Going to a Succeeding Line

Indented, italicized, lower-case paragraph   (Style 4)
heading, flush left and single-spaced when going
to a succeeding line, and ending with a period.

Figure 5. The Five APA Heading Styles.

Using One Heading Level

Table 1 shows the correct style for one heading level: APA style 1.

Table 1. Correct Style for One Heading Level.

LEVEL	APA STYLE	DESCRIPTION
1	1	Centered, With Initial Caps

Figure 6 shows an example of the heading style for one heading level. See Appendix A for a complete sample report with one heading level.

NOTE: *The title of the report is a first-level heading like the main headings of the report; therefore, it also uses Style 1.*

NOTE: *As mentioned on page 11, the title "Introduction" is not used in APA style, because this section is identified by its position in the document.*

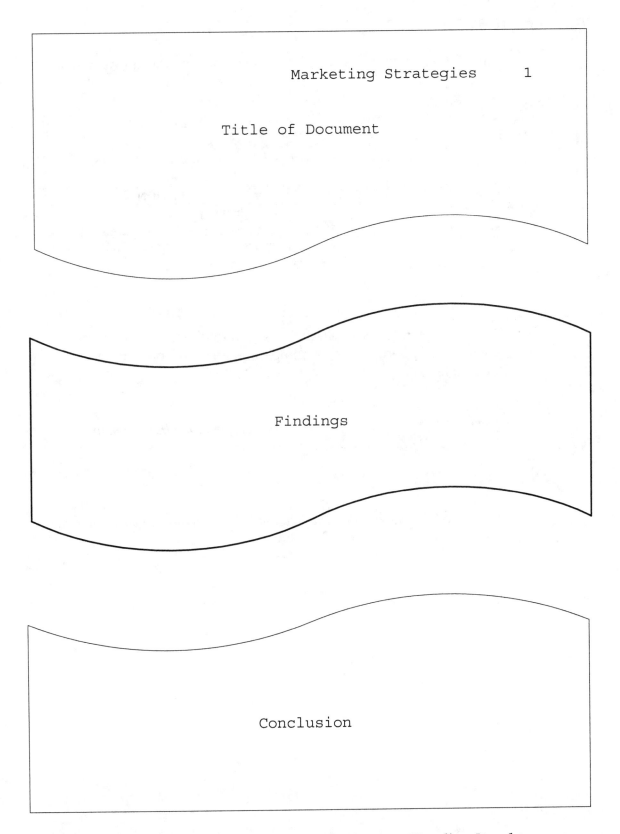

Figure 6. Example of the Style for One Heading Level.

Using Two Heading Levels

Table 2 shows the correct styles for two heading levels: APA styles 1 and 3.

Table 2. Correct Styles for Two Heading Levels.

LEVEL	APA STYLE	DESCRIPTION
1	1	Centered, With Initial Caps
2	3	*Flush Left, Italicized, With Initial Caps, and Single-spaced When Going to a Succeeding Line*

Figure 7 shows an example of the styles to use for two heading levels. See Appendix B for a complete sample report with two heading levels.

NOTE: *The title of the report is a first-level heading like the main headings of the report; therefore, it also uses Style 1.*

NOTE: *As mentioned on page 11, the title "Introduction" is not used in APA style, because this section is identified by its position in the document.*

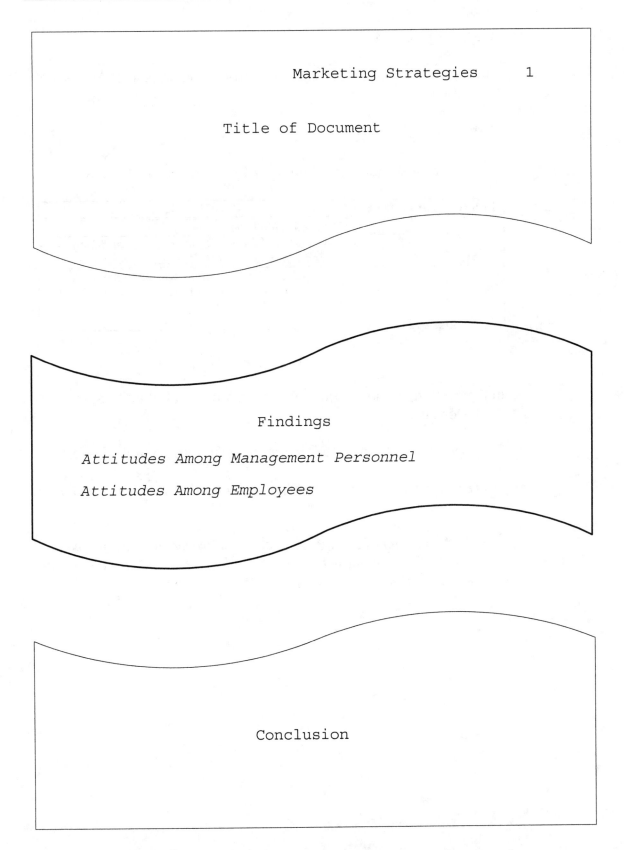

Figure 7. Example of the Styles for Two Heading Levels.

Using Three Heading Levels

Table 3 shows the correct styles for three heading levels: APA styles 1, 3, and 4:

Table 3. Correct Styles for Three Heading Levels.

LEVEL	APA STYLE	DESCRIPTION
1	1	Centered, With Initial Caps
2	3	*Flush Left, Italicized, With Initial Caps, and Single-spaced When Going to a Succeeding Line*
3	4	*Indented, italicized, with lower-case words, flush left and single-spaced when going to a second line, and ending with a period.*

In Figure 8, note the period at the end of the level three headings and the lower-case words.

See Appendix C for a complete sample with three heading levels.

NOTE: *The title of the report is a first-level heading just like the main headings of the report; therefore, it also uses Style 1.*

NOTE: *As mentioned on page 11, the title "Introduction" is not used in APA style, because this section is identified by its position in the document.*

Pros and Cons of Electronic Communication
At Two Large Companies

Types of Electronic Communication at Company A

E-mail

Pagers

Cell phones

> *Company-owned.*

> *Employee-owned.*

Fax machines

Types of Electronic Communication at Company B

E-mail

Pagers

Cell phones

> *Company-owned.*

> *Employee-owned.*

Fax machines

Conclusion

Figure 8. Example of the Styles for Three Heading Levels.

Using Four Heading Levels

Table 4 shows the correct styles for four heading levels: APA styles 1, 2, 3, and 4.

Table 4. Correct Styles for Four Heading Levels.

LEVEL	APA STYLE	DESCRIPTION
1	1	Centered, With Initial Caps
2	2	*Centered, Italicized, With Initial Caps*
3	3	*Flush Left, Italicized, With Initial Caps, and Single-spaced When Going to a Succeeding Line*
4	4	*Indented, italicized, with lower-case words, flush left and single-spaced when going to a second line, and ending with a period.*

Figure 9 shows four heading levels. This example is four levels because the Company-Owned and Employee-Owned headings have been divided further into subheadings. Note the lower-case letters on succeeding words of the fourth-level headings.

See Appendix D for a complete sample chapter with four heading levels.

NOTE: *The title of the report is a first-level heading just like the main headings of the report; therefore, it also uses Style 1.*

NOTE: *As mentioned on page 11, the title "Introduction" is not used in APA style, because this section is identified by its position in the document.*

*Types of Cell-Phones and Pagers Used
At Two Large Companies*

Types of Cell Phones and Pagers at Company A

Cell Phones

Company-Owned

Sprint.

AT&T.

Employee-Owned

Sprint.

AT&T.

Other brands.

Pagers

Types of Electronic Communication at Company B

Cell phones

Company-Owned

AT&T.

Other brands.

Employee-Owned

Cingular.

Nextel.

Conclusion

Figure 9. Example of the Styles for Four Heading Levels.

Using Five Heading Levels

Table 5 shows the correct style for five heading levels: APA styles 5, 1, 2, 3, and 4.

Table 5. Correct Styles for Five Heading Levels.

LEVEL	APA STYLE	DESCRIPTION
1	5	CENTERED, UPPERCASE
2	1	Centered, With Initial Caps
3	2	*Centered, Italicized, With Initial Caps*
4	3	*Flush Left, Italicized, With Initial Caps, and Single-spaced When Going to a Succeeding Line*
5	4	*Indented, italicized, with lower-case words, flush left and single-spaced when going to a second line, and ending with a period.*

Figure 10 shows an example of five heading levels. This example is five levels because the "Other Brands" heading has been divided further into the brand names.

See Appendix E for a complete sample report with five heading levels.

NOTE: *The title of a report is a level one heading just like the main headings of the report; therefore, it also uses Style 5.*

NOTE: *As mentioned on page 11, the title "Introduction" is not used in APA style, because this section is identified by its position in the document.*

TYPES OF CELL PHONES AND PAGERS USED

AT TWO LARGE COMPANIES

TYPES OF CELL PHONES AND PAGERS AT COMPANY A

Cell Phones

Company-owned

Sprint

AT&T

Employee-owned

Sprint

AT&T

Other brands

Nokia.

Emerson.

TYPES OF CELL PHONES AND PAGERS AT COMPANY B

Cell Phones

Company-owned

Sprint

AT&T

(And so on....)

Figure 10. Example of the Styles for Five Heading Levels.

Creating Body Text

Follow these rules when creating the body text:

1. Type your text double-spaced, printed on *one* side of the page.

CAUTION!

If you photocopy your document,
do *not* create a double-sided version!

---

2. Type approximately 25 lines per page. See Appendices A through E for sample pages.

3. Use a *ragged-right* margin for your pages. A ragged right margin has lines of differing length, as shown in Figure 11. Compare it to the example in Figure 12, which shows a *right-justified* margin.

    A right-justified margin makes the document more difficult to read because the computer adds extra spaces between the words to make the lines end evenly. If you look closely at the text in Figure 12, you can see those extra spaces. Ragged-right margins are kinder to your instructor's eyes.

4. Indent the first line of each paragraph five spaces.

5. Double-space between paragraphs—do not quadruple-space!

CAUTION!

Strict APA guidelines require no hyphenation in document text. This rule is meant to prevent problems when typesetting a document for the *APA Journal*. Check your school's or department's requirements before hyphenating any of your text.

Duis atem vel eum iriure dolor in hendrerit in vulputate velit esse molestie consequat, vel illum dolore eu feugiat nulla facilisis at vero eros et accumsan et iusto odio dignissim qui blandit praesent luptatum zzril delenit augue duis dolore te feugait nulla facilisi.

Figure 11. Example of Text With Ragged Right Margin.

Duis atem vel eum iriure dolor in hendrerit in vulputate velit esse molestie consequat, vel illum dolore eu feugiat nulla facilisis at vero eros et accumsan et iusto odio dignissim qui blandit praesent luptatum zzril delenit augue duis dolore te feugait nulla facilisi.

Figure 12. Example of Text With Justified Right Margin.

Formatting the Page Numbers

Strict APA rules state that you should number the body of your document with Arabic numerals starting from the title page. Place the page number about five spaces from the header. Figure 13 shows a sample of a first page of a report with the page number in the correct position.

Student APA rules allow the frontis material to be numbered with lower-case Roman numerals, however (title page through List of Tables in Table 6 below). Ask your professor which method he or she prefers.

Numbering the Pages

Number the pages of your document chronologically starting with the title page. This includes the frontis material and the appendices (see Chapter 6).

As a reminder, Table 6 shows how to number the pages of your document per the strict APA requirements (not the student instructions).

Table 6. Correct Page Numbering.

PAGES	STYLE OF NUMBER	STARTING NUMBER
Title page	Arabic numeral	1
Executive Summary*, **	Arabic numeral	2
Table of Contents*	Arabic numeral	3 or number following the Executive Summary
List of Figures*	Arabic numeral	Number following the Table of Contents
List of Tables*	Arabic numeral	Number following the List of Figures
Body	Arabic numeral	Number following the Table of Contents or List of Figures or Tables, whichever is last
Appendices*	Arabic numerals	Number following the last page of the body.

Optional and may not be required.
***If required, double-check to see if this is the location in which your professor wants the executive summary included in the paper.*

Reorganization Factors   1

Problems With Reorganization Factors

at ABC Company

Lorem ipsum dolor sit amet, consectetuer adipisci

elit, sed diam nonummy nibh eusmod tin cidunt ut loreet

dolore magna aliquam erat volutpat. Ut wisi ad minim

veniam, quis nostrud exerci tation ulcorper suscipit

lobortis nisl ut aliquip ex ea commodo consequat.

Duis atem vel eum iriure dolor in hendrerit in

putate velit esse molestie consequat, vel illum dolore

feugiat nulla facilisis at vero eros et accumsan et

odio dignissim qui blandit praesent luptatum zzril del

augue duis dolore te feugait nulla facilisi.

Nam liber tempor cum soluta nobis eleifend id

congue nihil imperdiet doming id quod mazim placerat

possim assum.

Lorem ipsum dolor sit amet, consectetuer adipisci

elit, sed diam nonummy nibh euismod tin cidunt ut loreet

dolore magna aliquam erat volutpat. Ut wisi enim minim

veniam, quis nostrud exerci tation ullamcorper.

Figure 13. Example of First Page of a Report Showing Page Numbering.*

* (This report has no title page)

Chapter 2

Placing Graphics

Graphics are very important in your document. The saying "A picture is worth a thousand words" is very true. Graphics help your readers understand information that is difficult to get across in words.

Your document can include two types of graphics:

- Figures

- Tables

This chapter explains how to place each of these on the page.

Placing Figures

Figures include diagrams, pictures, photos, line drawings, bar and line graphs, pie charts, etc. Do not include figures in your report unless they are absolutely necessary. If you include a figure, refer to it by number in your text:

`Figure 1 shows the Model 300 ergonomic desk.`

or

`The Model 300 ergonomic desk is available in`

`three styles (see Figure 1).`

Strict APA rules state that figures must be placed on separate pages at the back of the report. Student rules allow them to be merged into the document, however. Since you are doing a report for class and not for publication, your instructor may want you to follow the student format. If so, place them as closely as possible to where you reference them; that means on the same page if there is room or on the very next page.

Each figure must have a sequential number and a caption. The caption must be a complete sentence and should accurately describe the contents of the artwork. Strict APA rules state the maximum sizes your figure can be due to column limitations in the *APA Journal*. Since you are not submitting for publication, however, you are not so limited. Your figure can be narrower than the required margins of the page, but it cannot be wider.

Use a sans serif font like Helvetica, Ariel, Futura, Univers, Geneva, and Optima for any text in the figure itself (not the caption).

Number figures separately from tables; i.e., Figure 1, Figure 2, Figure 3, and Table 1, Table 2, Table 3—*not* Figure 1, Table 2, Figure 3. (For information on table placement, see *Placing Tables*, page 32.) Place the caption below the artwork, as shown in Figure 14.

Notice that the word "Figure" and the figure number are italicized, but that the caption itself is in plain type. A period follows the figure number. Note that the figure caption immediately follows the figure number and that when the caption goes onto a second line, it is double-spaced.

Ergonomic Needs of ABC Company   57

Lorem ipsum dolor sit amet, consectetuer adipiscing, sed nonummy nibh euismod tin cidunt ut laoreet dolore magna aliquam volutpat. Ut wisi enim ad minim veniam, quis nostrud exerci tation ullam corper suscipit lobortis nisl ut aliquip ex ea commodo.

Duis atem vel eum iriure dolor in hendrerit in vulputate velit esse molestie consequat, vel illum dolore eu feugiat nulla facilisi. Lorem ipsum dolor sit amet, consec-as shown in Figure 5:

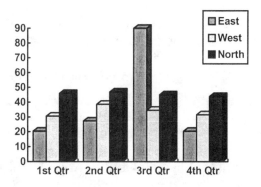

Figure 5. Nam liber tempor cum soluta nobis eleifend option congue nihil imperdiet doming id quod mazim placerat facer possim assum.

Figure 14. Example of Figure and Figure Caption Placement.

Placing Tables

Tables compare large amounts of data in columns. A table can be used to compare results in certain categories for test groups, for instance. Do not include a table unless absolutely necessary. If you include a table, refer to it by number in your text:

```
Table 4 shows the comparisons for the 10

test groups.
```

or

```
The comparisons for the 10 test groups

vary substantially (see Table 4).
```

Strict APA rules state that tables must be placed on separate pages at the back of the report. Student rules allow them to be merged into the document, however. Since you are doing a report for class and not for publication, your instructor may want you to follow the student format. If so, place them as closely as possible to where you reference them; that means on the same page if there is room or on the very next page.

Each table must have a sequential number and a caption. The caption must be a complete sentence and should accurately describe the contents of the artwork. Strict APA rules state the maximum sizes your table can be due to column limitations in the *APA Journal.* Since you are not submitting for publication, however, you are not so limited. Your table can be narrower than the required margins of the page, but it cannot be wider.

Use a sans serif font like Helvetica, Ariel, Futura, Univers, Geneva, and Optima for any text in the table itself (not the caption). Note that the label on the left axis is vertical.

Number tables sequentially, and separately from the figures; i.e., Table 1, Table 2, Table 3, and Figure 1, Figure 2, Figure 3—***not*** Table 1, Figure 2, Table 3. (For information on figure placement, see Placing Figures, page 30.) Place the caption at the top of the table, as shown in Figure 15.

Notice that the word "Table" and the number are in plain type, and that the caption itself is on the line *below* the word "Table." In addition, the caption is italicized—almost the opposite of the format for a figure caption. Note also that, like a figure caption, when the table caption goes onto a second line, it is double-spaced.

Ergonomic Needs of ABC Company   57

Lorem ipsum dolor sit amet, consectetuer adipiscing, sed nonummy nibh euismod tin cidunt ut laoreet dolore magna aliquam volutpat. Ut wisi enim ad minim veniam, quis nostrud exerci tation ullam corper.

Duis atem vel eum iriure dolor in hendrerit in vulputate velit esse molestie consequat, vel illum dolore eu consecatus as shown in Table 3:

Table 3

Nam liber tempor cum soluta nobis eleifend option congue nihil imperdiet doming id quod mazim placerat facer possim.

FEATURES

	Adj. Hght.	Kybd Tray	Book-shelf	Cup-brd.	Draw-ers	Chair incl.	Diff. Colors
ABC	X	X	X	X	X		X
XYZ		X		X	X	X	
ACME	X	X			X		
ACE		X	X		X		X

COMPANY

Nam liber tempor cum soluta nobis eleifend id congue nihil imperdiet doming id quod mazim placerat possim assum.

Figure 15. Example of Table and Table Caption Placement.

Numbering Figures and Tables in the Appendices

When you number figures and tables in the appendices, you must include the appendix letter in the numbering; i.e., Figure A1, Figure A2, Figure B1, Figure B2, Table A1, Table B1, etc. (See Chapter 6, *Formatting the Frontis Material and Appendices.*) Once again, the lists of figures and tables must be separate.

Chapter 3

Formatting Mathematical and Statistical Material

If you are writing a comprehensive report, you may need to include other kinds of information, such as:

- mathematical symbols or equations

- statistical material

This chapter explains how to format your statistics per the APA style guide. It assumes that you already understand and have performed statistical analyses.

Formatting Mathematical Material

Citing statistical and mathematical references is easiest when using a computer. Most word processing programs have a Symbol font that allows you to place any statistical or mathematical symbol on the page.

This section shows you how to format:

- equations

- displayed equations in the text

- superscripted characters

- subscripted characters

Formatting an Equation

When you type short and simple mathematical copy, space it out just the way you would a sentence with words, as shown in Figure 16. Place it all on one line, using brackets and parentheses to make the related parts of the equation clear to the reader.

Notice that there are no spaces between brackets and parentheses or between parentheses and the first number, but there are spaces between the other elements of the equation. Study these examples closely for spacing requirements and for italicized elements.

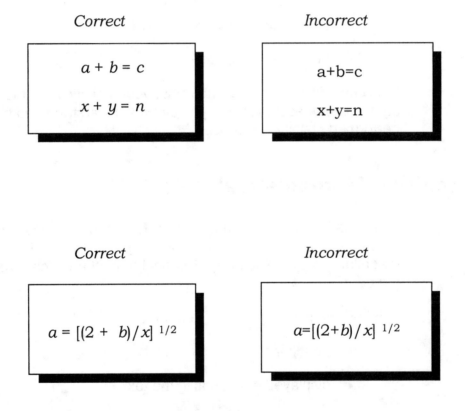

Figure 16. How to Type Mathematical Copy.

Formatting a Displayed Equation in the Text

When an equation takes up more than one line of space, you must place it by itself, just as you would a figure or table. Skip two lines before and after the equation. Figure 17 shows an example.

Number displayed equations consecutively, and place the number in parentheses at the right margin. When referring to the equation in the text, refer to it as "Equation *n*" (i.e., the word "Equation" and then its number). For example, the equation in Figure 18 would be referred to as Equation 1.

```
     Lorem ipsum dolor sit amet, consectateur

adipiscing elit, sed diam nonummy nibh euismod

tin cidunt dolore magna aliquam erat voluptat:


                        2 + b
        b =                                     (1)
                         x



     Duis atem vel eum iriure dolor in hendrerit

in vulputate vlit esse molestie consequat, vel

illum dolore eu feugiat nulla facilisis at vero

eros et accumsan et iusto.
```

Figure 17. Placement of a Displayed Equation in the Text.

Formatting a Superscripted Character

A "superscripted" character is raised above the normal line of the text. Figure 18 shows Einstein's famous equation, which has a superscripted "2" on the MC. Most word processors have a superscript command to allow automatic placement of these characters.

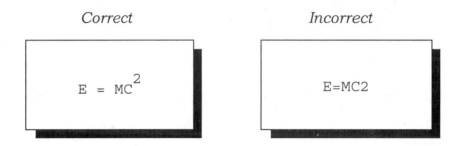

Figure 18. Correct Format for a Superscripted Character.

Formatting a Subscripted Character

A "subscripted" character is dropped below the normal line of the text. Figure 19 shows the chemical composition of water; it has a subscripted "2" between the "H" and "O." Most word processors have a superscript command to allow automatic placement of these characters.

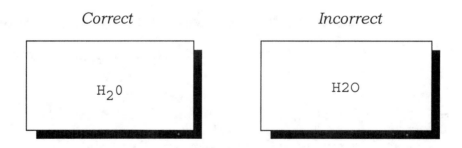

Figure 19. Correct Format for a Subscripted Character.

Formatting Statistical Material

When formatting statistical material, follow these few simple rules:

1. If the statistic is common one, you need not include the reference for it. Include the reference only if the statistic is new or used in a controversial way.

2. If the formula for the statistic is a common one, do not include it in your text. Give formulas only for statistics that are new or rare, or extremely essential to your document.

This section shows you how to format:

- Inferential statistics

- Observed statistics

- Sample statistics

- Subject statistics

Formatting Inferential Statistics

There are three types of inferential statistics:

- t tests

- F tests

- chi-square tests

When you format any of these types of statistics, be sure to include enough information so the reader can corroborate your analyses.

Formatting *t* test Statistics

Format *t* test statistics as shown in Figure 20. Notice that the "t" is italicized and is lower case. Place spaces only before and after the equal sign.

$$t(50) = 1.5$$

Figure 20. Example of the Formatting for a t test Statistic.

Formatting *F* test Statistics

Format *F* test statistics as shown in Figure 21. In this example, there are two *F* test statistics; hence, "*F*s" rather than "*F*." Notice that the "*F*" is italicized and is upper case. Pay close attention to the spacing.

$$Fs(3, 125) = 4.25 \text{ and } 3.95$$

Figure 21. Example of the Formatting for an F test Statistic.

Formatting Chi-Square Statistics

Format chi-square test statistics as shown in Figure 22. Place the degrees of freedom and sample size in parentheses. Notice that the "*N*" is upper case and the "*p*" is lower case and that both are italicized. Pay close attention to the spacing.

$$\chi^2(6, N = 300) = 8.57, p < .05$$

Figure 22. Example of the Formatting for a Chi-Square Statistic.

Formatting Observed Statistics

Observed statistics, which may be sample statistics, are shown by using lower-case Greek letters. Figure 23 shows an example. The "χ^2" represents the observed-type sample statistic.

$$\chi^2(6, N = 300) = 8.57, p < .05$$

Figure 23. Example of the Formatting for Observed Statistics.

Formatting Sample Statistics

Sample statistics are expressed by using Latin letters, such as "SD" for Standard Deviation. An example is shown in Figure 24.

$$SD = 5.45$$

Figure 24. Example of the Formatting for Sample Statistics.

Formatting Subject Statistics

Point out the number of subjects in a total sample by using an upper-case, italicized "*N*." Use a lower-case, italicized "*n*" to represent the number of subjects in a portion of the total sample. Figure 25 shows some examples. The number "350" represents the total sample; therefore, the capital "*N*" is used. The number "20" represents a portion of that sample; therefore, the lower-case "*n*" is used.

$$N = 350$$

$$n = 20$$

Figure 25. Examples of the Formatting for Subject Statistics.

Formatting Statistical Symbols

Refer to Table 7 if you are not sure how to format a particular statistical symbol.

Table 7. Statistical Abbreviations and Symbols

SYMBOL	DEFINITION	SYMBOL	DEFINITION
A_2	Control chart factor for means	H	Kruskal-Wallis test statistic
a	Y-intercept	H_0	Null hypothesis under test
A.D.	Average deviation	H_1	Alternative hypothesis
ANCOVA	Analysis of covariance	HSD	Tukey *a* procedure
ANOVA	Analysis of variance	k	Coefficient of alienation
b	Slope of the regression line	k^2	Coefficient of nondetermination
c	Mean number of defects per unit	K-R 20	Kuder-Richardson formula
$_nC_r$	Combination of *n* things taken at *r* time	LR	Likelihood ratio (used with some chi-squares
χ^2	Chi-square statistic	LSD	Fisher's least significant difference
C.V.	Coefficient of variation	M	Mean (arithmetic average)
CPI	Consumer Price Index	MANOVA	Multivariate analysis of variance
d	Cohen's measure of effect size	Mdn	Median
d'	(*d* prime) measure of sensitivity	mle	Maximum likelihood estimate
D	Used in Kolmogorov-Smirnov test	MS	Mean square
D_4	Control limit factor for the range	MSE	Mean square error
df	Degree of freedom	$MSTR$	Mean square treatment
EMV	Expected monetary value	n	Number of items in subsample
EQL	Expected opportunity loss	N	Total number in a sample
EVPI	Expected value of perfect information	ns	Nonsignificant
f	Frequency	$_nP_r$	Permutation of *n* things taken *r* at a time
f_e	Expected frequency	ρ_c	Weighted mean of sample proportions
f_o	Observed frequency	ρ	Proportion of success in a sample
F	Fisher's *F* ratio	p	Probability
F_{max}	Hartley's test of variance homogeneity	P	Percentage, percentile
g	Hedge's measure of effect size	P	Price index
G.M.	Geometric mean	$P(A)$	Probability of an event happening

Table 7. Statistical Abbreviations and Symbols, Cont'd.

SYMBOL	DEFINITION	SYMBOL	DEFINITION
$P(A/B)$	Probability of an event given that another event has happened	SS total	Sum of squares total
pr	Partial correlation	SSB	Sum of squares blocks
Q	Quartile	SSE	Sum of squares error
Q_1	First quartile	SSR	Sum of squares regression
Q_3	Third quartile	SST	Sum of squares treatments
Q	Quantity index	t	Computed value of *t* test
$Q.D.$	Quartile deviation	T	Computed value of Wilcoxon's or McCall's test
r	Pearson product-moment correlation	T^2	Computed value of Hotelling's test
r^2	Pearson product-moment correlation squared; coefficient of deviation	Tukey a	Tukey's HSD procedure
r_b	Biserial correlation	U	Mann-Whitney U statistic
r_k	Reliability of mean *k* judges' rating	V	Value index
r_1	Estimate reliability of the typical judge	W	Kendall's coefficient of concordance
r_{pb}	Point-biserial correlation	x	Abscissa (horizontal axis in graph)
r_s	Spearman rank correlation coefficient	X_o	Control limit for sample mean
R	Multiple correlation; composite rank	X_w	Weighted mean
R^2	Multiple correlation squared; measure of strength of relationship	X	Sample mean
s_d	Standard deviation of paired differences	Y	Predicted value of Y
s^2	Sample variance	y	Ordinate (vertical axis in graph)
$s_{y'x}$	Standard error of estimate	z	Standard score; difference between one value in a distribution and the mean of the distribution divided by the SD
s	Sample standard deviation	$|a|$	Absolute value of *a*
sk	Coefficient of skewness	μ	Population mean
SD	Standard deviation	ρ	Population coefficient of correlation
SE	Standard error (of measurement)	σ^2	Population variance
SEM	Standard error of measurement	σ_p	Standard error of the proportion
SEM	Structural equation modeling	σ	Population standard deviation
sr	Semipartial correlation	σ_2	Standard error of the mean

Chapter 4

Using Seriation and Abbreviations

Using Seriation

No doubt you will have paragraphs in your text in which you wish to state a number of points, such as a list or a set of steps, or other text that is in *series* form; hence, the word *seriation*. You can create these in three forms:

- As a list in a sentence

- As a series of steps

- As a list of points

Numbering the Parts of a Series in a Paragraph or Sentence

Here's how you number the parts of a series in a sentence. Figure 26 shows how your sentence should look. When the parts (phrases) do not have commas within themselves, note that lower-case letters in parentheses are used and that commas, not semicolons, appear after each phrase.

```
Duis atem vel eum iriure dolor in hendrerit in

vulputate (a) velit essemolestie consequat, (b) vel

illum dolore eu feugiat nulla facilisis at vero eros

et accumsan, and (c) iusto odio dignissim qui blandit

praesent luptatum zzril delenit augue duis dolore te

feugait nulla acilisi.
```

Figure 26. Example of a List in a Sentence.

When the phrases you use do have internal commas, however, you must use semicolons to separate them as shown in Figure 27. This example also shows the list beginning after a colon. In that case, the first word of the list must have an initial capital letter.

```
Duis atem vel eum iriure dolor in hendrerit in

vulputate: (a) Velit essemolestie consequat, dolor

in hendrerit; (b) vel illum dolore eu feugiat nulla

facilisis at vero eros et accumsan, odio dignissim

qui; and (c) iusto odio dignissim qui blandit

praesent luptatum zzril delenit, augue duis dolore

te feugait nulla acilisi.
```

Figure 27. Example of a List in a Sentence Containing Commas in the Phrases.

Creating Steps in a Procedure

To create steps in a procedure, format your text as shown in Figure 28. Note that each step is indented five spaces, while the second and succeeding lines are indented further to line up with the first word in the first line.

```
Duis atem vel eum iriure dolor in hendrerit:
    1. Vulputate velit esse molestie consequat, vel
       illum dolore eu feugiat nulla facilisis at
       vero eros et accumsan et iusto.
    2. Odio dignissim qui blandit praesent luptatum
       zzril delenit augue duis dolore te feugait
       nulla facilis.
    3. Nam liber tempor cum soluta nobis eleifend
       option congue nihil imperdiet doming id quod
       mazim placerat facer possim assum.
    4. Lorem ipsum dolor sit amet, consectetuer
       adipiscing elit, sed diam nonummy nibh euismod
       tin cidunt ut laoreet dolore magna aliquam
       erat volutpat.
    5. Ut wisi enim ad minim veniam, quis nostrud
       exerci tation ullamcorper suscipit lobortis
       nisl ut aliquip ex ea commodo consequat.
```

Figure 28. Example of Steps in a Procedure.

Using Abbreviations

There are two types of abbreviations:

- Latin abbreviations

- Scientific abbreviations

The only rules to remember are:

1. Never start a sentence with a lower-case abbreviation or a symbol that stands alone.

2. Instead, capitalize the abbreviation or acronym, and capitalize the first letter of a word attached to a symbol.

Using Latin Abbreviations

Use the Latin abbreviations shown in Table 8 in parenthetical material only. Be sure to include the periods and commas as shown in this table and to avoid spaces between the elements of the abbreviation.

Use the full English meaning when referring to these items in non-parenthetical material.

As with any rule, there are exceptions. You can use the Latin abbreviations shown in Table 9 in both parenthetical and non-parenthetical material.

Table 8. Latin Abbreviations Used in Parenthetical Material and Their Meanings.

ABBREVIATION	MEANING	ABBREVIATION	MEANING
cf.	compare	i.e.,	that is
e.g.,	for example	viz.,	namely
, etc.	, and so forth	vs.	versus, against

Table 9. Latin Abbreviations Used in Both Parenthetical and Non-Parenthetical Material.

ABBREVIATION	MEANING	WHERE USED
v.	versus	In references and text citations of court cases
et al.	and others	In the reference list and in the text

Using Scientific Abbreviations

Scientic abbreviations that may be used with the APA style fall into four main categories:

- Units of measure

- Chemical compounds

- Medical percentage concentrations

- Medical routes of administration

Using Abbreviations for Units of Measure

Table 10 shows the abbreviations for the units of measure and their meanings. Use these abbreviations and symbols for metric and nonmetric units of measure that are accompanied by numbers (e.g., 10 cm, 25° C, 18 hr). When they are not accompanied by numbers, use the full English meaning instead.

Using Abbreviations for Chemical Compounds

Refer to chemical compounds by their common or chemical name. If you use the common name, place the chemical name in parentheses. Refrain from using chemical formulas, even if they are shorter.

If the name of an organic compound is listed as an abbreviation or acronym in the *Webster's Collegiate Dictionary* (such as "DNA" for "deoxyribonucleic acid"), you can use it without explaining its meaning.

Table 10. Abbreviations for Units of Measure.

ABBREV.	MEANING	ABBREV.	MEANING
A	ampere	mA	milliampere
Å	angstrom	mEq	milliequivalent
AC	alternating current	meV	million electron volts
a.m.	ante meridiem	mg	milligram
°C	degrees Celsius	min	minute
Ci	curie	ml	milliliter
cm	centimeter	mm	millimeter
cps	cycles per second	mM	millimolar
dB	decibel (specify scale)	mmHg	millimeters of mercury
DC	direct current	mmol	millimole
deg/s	degrees per second	mol wt	molecular weight
dl	deciliter	mph	miles per hour (convert to metric)
°F	degrees Fahrenheit	ms	millisecond
g	gram	MΩ	megohm
g	gravity	N	newton
hr	hour	ns	nanosecond
Hz	hertz	p.m.	post meridiem
in.	inch	ppm	parts per million
IQ	intelligence quotient	psi	pound per square inch (convert to metric)
IU	international unit	rpm	revolutions per minute
kg	kilogram	s	second
km	kilometer	S	siemens
kph	kilometers per hour	V	volt
kW	kilowatt	W	watt
L	Liter	m	micrometer
m	meter		

Using Abbreviations in Concentrations

Specify solutions expressed as percentage concentrations rather than molar as a:

- weight per volume ratio (wt/vol)

- volume ratio (vol/vol)

- weight ratio (wt/wt) of solution to solvent

Be sure to use a ratio for concentrations of alcohol, glucose, and sucrose. Also specify the salt form (*d*-amphetamine HCl or *d*-amphetamine SO_4. Using a chemical name with a formula is allowed in this case:

10% (vol/vol) ethyl alcohol solution

Using Abbreviations in Routes of Administration

Abbreviate routes of administration only when they are accompanied by number-and-unit combinations. Do not use periods. Table 11 shows some examples.

Table 11. Examples of Abbreviations for Routes of Administration.

ABBREVIATION	EXPLANATION
icv	Intracerebral ventricular
im	Intramuscular
ip	Intraperitoneal
iv	Intravenous
sc	Subcutaneous

Using Abbreviations in Tables

You can use abbreviations, such as for the months of the year, in tables. Use the three-letter abbreviation, such as "Jan," "Feb," "Mar," etc. When referring to units of time in the text, however, spell them out completely, even when accompanied by a number (e.g., March 7, *not* Mar 7).

Using an Acronym

Acronyms are words formed from the initials of long terms, such as "TQM" for "Total Quality Management." Plan to use acronyms only for long, well-known terms. Spell out the phrase completely the first time you use it, and put the acronym in parentheses, as shown in Figure 29. The next time you refer to this term, use the acronym by itself.

Duis atem vel eum iriure dolor in hendrerit in

vulputate velit essemolestie consequat, vel illum

dolore eu feugiat nulla facilisis at vero eros et

accumsan, and is called Total Quality Management

(TQM). Dignissim qui blandit praesent luptatum zzril

delenit augue duis dolore te feugait nulla acilisi.

Figure 29. Example of the First Use of an Acronym.

Formatting Plurals

To create a plural of an acronym, abbreviation, or statistical symbol, just add "s." Do not include an apostrophe. Table 12 shows some examples.

Table 12. Examples of Plurals of Abbreviations.

ABBREVIATION	EXPLANATION
IQs	Intelligence quotients
Eds.	Editors, Editions
vols.	Volumes

There are two exceptions, in which no "s" is added:

- "pp." is the correct plural for "pages"

- Units of measure do not use an "s"

Using Abbreviations in the Reference List

You can use abbreviations in the Reference list in two ways:

- For parts of books and other publications

- To indicate the state in which a publisher is located

Using Abbreviations for Parts of Books and Other Publications

You can use the abbreviations in Table 13 to indicate parts of books and other publications.

Table 13. Abbreviations Used in the Reference List to Indicate Parts of Books and Other Publications.

ABBREVIATION	MEANING	ABBREVIATION	MEANING
chap.	chapter	p. (pp.)	page (pages)
ed.	edition	Vol.	Volume
Rev. ed.	revised edition	Vols.	Volumes
2nd ed.	second edition	No.	Number
Ed. (Eds.)	Editor (Editors)	Pt.	Part
Trans.	Translator(s)	Tech. Rep.	Technical Report
n.d.	no date	Suppl.	Supplement

Using Abbreviations to Indicate the Location of the Publisher

When referencing books in the Reference list, you must include the city where the publisher is located. If the city is not a major one (see Table 15, page 141), you must include the two-letter postal state code abbreviation, as shown in Table 14, or the country name. Do not type a period after these abbreviations.

Table 14. Two-letter Postal Code Abbreviations for States and Territories Used in Book References.

LOCATION	ABBREVIATION	LOCATION	ABBREVIATION
Alabama	AL	Missouri	MO
Alaska	AK	Montana	MT
American Samoa	AS	Nebraska	NE
Arizona	AZ	Nevada	NV
Arkansas	AR	New Hampshire	NH
California	CA	New Jersey	NJ
Canal Zone	CZ	New Mexico	NM
Colorado	CO	New York	NY
Connecticut	CT	North Carolina	NC
Delaware	DE	North Dakota	ND
District of Columbia	DC	Ohio	OH
Florida	FL	Oklahoma	OK
Georgia	GA	Oregon	OR
Guam	GU	Pennsylvania	PA
Hawaii	HI	Puerto Rico	PR
Idaho	ID	Rhode Island	RI
Illinois	IL	South Carolina	SC
Indiana	IN	South Dakota	SD
Iowa	IA	Tennessee	TN
Kansas	KS	Texas	TX
Kentucky	KY	Utah	UT
Louisiana	LA	Vermont	VT
Maine	ME	Virginia	VA
Maryland	MD	Virgin Islands	VI
Massachusetts	MA	Washington	WA
Michigan	MI	West Virginia	WV
Minnesota	MN	Wisconsin	WI
Mississippi	MS	Wyoming	WY

Chapter 5

Documenting Your Sources in the Text

During the course of writing your document, you will research many books, magazine articles, and other publications, and perhaps conduct interviews with experts in your topic. Any time you use that material in your document, you must credit the source; otherwise, you are committing plagiarism.

The APA employs a specific method for documenting sources. You must first cite the source in the text, where the borrowed material appears, then again in the list of references that follows the last page. This chapter explains how to create the in-text citations.

There are three types of in-text citations:

- *Paraphrased material*

  Perhaps you have read a book or article, or even several books or articles, and you are discussing the idea or ideas contained therein. You have not used any of the author's wording, but have explained the concepts in your own words.

- *Quotes of fewer than 40 words*

  An author's words say what you want to say, so you use those exact words. You quote fewer than 40 words from the article or book.

- *Quotes of 40 words or more*

  Here again, you use the author's words, but this time you quote 40 words or more of the book or article.

Because the ideas in paraphrased material and quotations are not your own, you must credit their sources. The APA style does *not* use footnotes for citations. Instead, sources are credited by using what are called "parenthetical citations."

NOTE: *The citations contained in this section are not necessarily real; they have been created for example purposes.*

Citing Paraphrased Material

You can paraphrase material in two different ways:

- When you do not name the author in your sentence

- When you name the author in your sentence

Paraphrasing Material Without Naming the Author in the Sentence

With some paraphrased material, you may just state the concept; for example, perhaps you want to explain Alvin Toffler's concept of our technological future without directly quoting from his book or stating his name in the text of the sentence itself. The correct way to credit the source of this information is to type the author's last name, a comma, a space, then the year of publication, as shown in Figure 30, so the reader will know what to look up in the reference list. Cite a magazine article the same way.

Compare these citations to those in which the author's name does appear in the text of the sentence (see page 58).

Including a Page Number

If you are paraphrasing material from a specific page or magazine article, you may even wish to include a page number, as shown in Figure 31. After the year, add a comma, a space, then a lower-case "p," a period, another space, and the page number.

Including a Range of Pages

Cite a range of pages as shown in Figure 32. Note that you must use the plural form "pp." rather than the singular form "p."

As global conflicts fade in the East/West and North/ South, and society continues to undergo rapid technological change, the world will experience a deepening split between the "fast" and the "slow"; this constitutes a new division that is far more important (Toffler, 1990).

Figure 30. Example of an In-Text Citation of Paraphrased Material Without Using the Author's Name in the Sentence.

As society continues to undergo rapid technological change, people suffer from what we now call "future shock" (Jones, 1993, p. 24).

Figure 31. Example of an In-Text Citation of Paraphrased Material From a Specific Page or Magazine Article Without Using the Author's Name in the Sentence and Showing a Page Number.

By the year 2000, 95% of all offices will use PCs (Jones, 1993, pp. 24-30).

Figure 32. Example of an In-Text Citation of Paraphrased Material Without Using the Author's Name in the Sentence and Covering a Range of Pages.

Paraphrasing Material and Naming the Author in the Sentence

You may paraphrase material and include the author's name as part of your sentence, but you must still let the reader know from which publication the information came. Cite the source as shown in Figure 33.

Notice that the parenthetical citation includes just the year (and page number, if applicable) and is next to the author's name, not at the end of the sentence.

Compare these citations to those in which the author's name does not appear in the text of the sentence (see page 56).

Including a Page Number

If you are paraphrasing material from a specific page or magazine article, you may even wish to include a page number, as shown in Figure 34. After the year, add a comma, a space, then a lower-case "p," a period, another space, and the page number.

Including a Range of Pages

Cite a range of pages as shown in Figure 35. Note that you must use the plural form "pp." rather than the singular form "p."

```
Toffler (1971) states that as society continues to
undergo rapid technological change, people will suffer
from "future shock."
```

Figure 33. Example of an In-Text Citation of Paraphrased Material Using the Author's Name in the Sentence.

```
According to Jones (1993, p. 24), as society continues
to undergo rapid technological change, people will
suffer from what we now call "future shock."
```

Figure 34. Example of an In-Text Citation of Paraphrased Material From a Specific Page or Magazine Article Using the Author's Name in the Sentence and Showing a Page Number.

```
Jones (1993, pp. 24-30) states that by the year 2005,
95% of all offices will use PCs.
```

Figure 35. Example of an In-Text Citation of Paraphrased Material Using the Author's Name in the Sentence and Covering a Range of Pages.

Citing Quotes

When you use direct quotations from people, the way you cite them depends on their length:

- Up to 40 words of manuscript text

- More than 40 words of manuscript text

Citing Up to 40 Words of Manuscript Text

Direct quotes that are up to 40 words of manuscript text are cited as part of the regular double-spaced text, as shown in Figure 36. Place the material in quotation marks to indicate that it is indeed a quote, rather than a paraphrase. Note that the citation is part of the sentence—the period is placed at the end of the entire sentence, *not* after the quotation.

In his book *Innovation and Entrepreneurship*, Peter Drucker (1985, p. 20) defines innovation as "the specific tool of entrepreneurs, the means by which they exploit change as an opportunity for a different business or a different service."

or

Peter Drucker (1985, p. 20) defines innovation as "the specific tool of entrepreneurs, the means by which they exploit change as an opportunity for a different business or a different service."

or

"Innovation is the specific tool of entrepreneurs, the means by which they exploit change as an opportunity for a different business or a different service" (Drucker, 1985, p. 20).

Figure 36. Correct Way to Cite Up to 40 Words of Manuscript Text.

Citing 40 Words or More of Manuscript Text

When a quote takes up 40 words or more of manuscript text, indent it five spaces and double-space it, as shown in Figure 37.

The first example in Figure 37 begins the quotation with a capital "I" because it begins a sentence. Examples 2 and 3 are continuations of the sentence begun above the quote, and so start with a lower-case letter. Notice also that in Example 2, the page number does not appear within the parenthetical material by the author's name, but, rather, in parentheses at the end of the quotation itself. Note that the form and placement of the citation depends on whether or not the author's name is used in the sentence.

Try to keep quotations to no more than 10 lines—figure out a way to paraphrase the material rather than lifting several pages wholesale from the original document.

```
Drucker (1985, p. 20) states that:

    Innovation is the specific tool of entrepreneurs,

    the means by which they exploit change as an

    opportunity for a different business or a different

    service. Entrepreneurs need to search purposefully

    for the sources of innovation, the changes and

    their symptoms that indicate opportunities for

    successful innovation.
```

Figure 37. Correct Way to Cite 40 Words or More of Manuscript Text.

or

> Drucker (1985) defines innovation as:
>
> > the specific tool of entrepreneurs, the means
> >
> > by which they exploit change as an opportunity
> >
> > for a different business or a different service.
> >
> > Entrepreneurs need to search purposefully for
> >
> > the sources of innovation, the changes and their
> >
> > symptoms that indicate opportunities for
> >
> > successful innovation (p. 20).

or

> Innovation is defined as:
>
> > the specific tool of entrepreneurs, the means
> >
> > by which they exploit change as an opportunity
> >
> > for a different business or a different service.
> >
> > Entrepreneurs need to search purposefully for
> >
> > the sources of innovation, the changes and their
> >
> > symptoms that indicate opportunities for
> >
> > successful innovation (Drucker, 1985, p. 20).

Figure 37. Correct Way to Cite 40 Words or More of Manuscript Text, Cont'd.

Citing a Publication with Two Authors

If more than one person has written the book or article, cite it as shown in Figure 38.

When the author's names appear in the parenthetical citation, use an *ampersand* (the "&" character) instead of the word "and" between the authors' names. Use the word "and" only when the authors' names appear as part of the actual text of the sentence.

Smith and Jones (1993, p. 137) stated that "by the year 2000, 95% of offices will use PCs."

or

In 1993, Smith and Jones (p. 137) stated that "by the year 2000, 95% of offices will use PCs."

or

"By the year 2000, 95% of offices will use PCs" (Smith & Jones, 1993, p. 137).

Figure 38. Examples of a Citation of a Publication With Two Authors.

Citing a Publication With Three or More Authors

Publications with three or more authors are cited according to the number of authors:

- Three, four, or five authors

- Six or more authors

If the work has three, four, or five authors, list all the authors the first time you cite the reference, as shown in Figure 39. Thereafter, cite it with the first author's name, followed by the Latin abbreviation "et al.," which means "and everyone" (see Figure 40).

NOTE: *For subsequent citations after the first citation in a paragraph, omit the year.*

```
The United States will be completely out of the

recession by 1997 (Everett, Jones & Sanders, 1993).
```

Figure 39. Example of a Citation of a Publication With Three-to-Five Authors.

If the work has six or more authors, cite it as shown in Figure 40 each time.

```
The United States entered another recession in the

middle of 2001 (Everett et al., 2002).
```

Figure 40. Example of a Subsequent Occurrence of a Citation With Three-to-Five Authors and All Citations With Six or More Authors.

EXCEPTION: *If you have two similar references with the same year, cite the last names of the first authors and as many of the subsequent authors as needed to make the one citation clearly distinguishable from the other.*

Citing Multiple Works

Cite several studies or works that all have the same common thread, philosophy, concepts, or conclusions as shown in Figure 41. List the authors in alphabetical order, using a semicolon between each of the citations.

```
Several studies (Chan & Jefferson, 1985; Gomez, 1989;

Thompson, 1992) show that....
```

Figure 41. Example of a Citation of Multiple Works.

Citing an Author with More Than One Publication in the Same Year

What if an author has more than one publication in the same year? Since the reader must be able to tell which listing in the list of references matches that particular citation, add a lower-case letter extension to each of the citations. Let's say Dylan Johnson wrote three books in 1998. Cite the first one as "1998a," as shown in Figure 42. Label Johnson's succeeding references "b," "c," etc., in the order of their citation in the text.

```
In PCs Today, Johnson (1998a) states that....
```

or

```
Johnson (1998a) states that....
```

or

```
As society continues to undergo rapid technological

change, people suffer from what Toffler calls "future

shock" (Johnson, 1998a, p. 24).
```

or

```
By the year 2005, 95% of all offices will use PCs

(Johnson, 1998a, pp. 24-25).
```

Figure 42. Examples of a Citation of a Publication by an Author With More Than One Publication in the Same Year.

Citing a Personal Communication

You may interview an expert or other relevant person face-to-face or by telephone during the course of your research, or you may receive a fax, letter, or e-mail from that person. If you use any portion of these communications, you must cite them in the text. Figure 43 shows an example of a citation for these sources. Give both the initials and the last name of the person involved. Use the words "personal communication" for all of these types of communications.

NOTE: *These sources are cited in the text but not included in the reference list because they do not provide recoverable data.*

```
According to J. D. Smith (personal communication,

November 15, 1995), management style . . . .
```

or

```
. . . with personnel problems (J. D. Smith, personal

communication, November 15, 1995)
```

Figure 43. Examples of a Citation of a Personal Communication.

Citing Legal Material

Your citations may include legal material. Legal material includes:

- Patents

- Court cases

- Statutes

- Testimony at hearings

- Full hearings

- Unenacted federal bills and resolutions

- Enacted bills and resolutions,

- Federal reports and documents

- Administrative and executive materials

Just like books and magazine articles, you must cite legal material in the text; however, it is documented in a slightly different way.

Citing a Patent

Cite a patent as follows depending on whether the patent number is used in the text of your sentence. The first example in Figure 44 shows the patent citation format when the patent number is used in the sentence. The second example in Figure 44 shows the patent citation format when the patent number is not used in the sentence:

```
Thomas Midgley, Jr.'s first patent was U.S. Patent No.
1,501,568 (1924), for an Aniline injector.
```

or

```
Thomas Midgley, Jr., received his first patent (U.S.
Patent No. 1,501,568, 1924) for his Aniline injector.
```

Figure 44. Examples of a Citation of a Patent.

Citing Court Cases

You can cite several types of court cases:

- Court decisions

- Unpublished cases

- Court cases at the trial level

- Court cases at the appellate level

All court cases are cited in the same manner, as shown in Figure 45. Be sure to underline the case title. Note that "v." is used, not the word "versus" or the abbreviation "vs.," and that the "v" is lower case.

The case of *Smith v. Jones* (1992) set a major legal precedent regarding sexual harassment in the workplace.

or

Apple Computer Company charged Microsoft Corporation with patent infringement, saying that Microsoft appropriated the code for its graphic interface and used it to development its Windows program (*Apple Computer v. Microsoft*, 1993).

Figure 45. Examples of a Citation of a Court Case.

Citing a Statute

When you cite a statute in the text, you must give the:

- name of the act

- year it was passed

You can do this in two ways, as shown in Figure 46. Be sure to use initial caps on each word of the statute.

```
To prevent people with disabilities from being

discriminated against in the workplace and in

society at large, the U.S. Congress passed the

Americans With Disabilities Act (1990).
```

or

```
To prevent people with disabilities from being

discriminated against in the workplace and in

society at large, the U.S. Congress passed the

Americans With Disabilities Act of 1990.
```

Figure 46. Examples of a Citation of a Statute.

Citing Testimony at Hearings

When you cite testimony from a hearing in the text of your document, you must:

- indicate that it is testimony

- include the name of the person testifying

- include the year in which the testimony took place

Figure 47 shows two examples. Note that the words "Testimony of John Smith" are italicized.

```
As Ronald Chesemore testified in RU486: The Import Ban
(1990), ut wisi enim ad minim veniam, quis nostrud
exerci tation ullamcorper suscipit lobortis nisl ut
aliquip.
```

or

```
''Lorem ipsum dolor sit amet, consectetuer adipiscing
elit, sed diam nonummy nibh euismod tin cidunt ut
laoreet dolore magna aliquam erat volutpat'' (RU486:
The Import Ban, 1990).
```

Figure 47. Examples of a Citation of Testimony at a Hearing.

Citing a Full Hearing

When you cite information from a full hearing in the text of your document, you must include the:

- name of the hearing

- year in which the hearing took place

Figure 48 shows two examples.

Note that the title of the hearing is italicized.

In the hearing *RU486: The Import Ban* (1990), ut wisi enim ad minim veniam, quis nostrud exerci tation ullamcorper suscipit lobortis nisl ut aliquip.

or

Lorem ipsum dolor sit amet, consectetuer adipiscing elit, sed diam nonummy nibh euismod tin cidunt ut laoreet dolore magna aliquam erat volutpat (*RU486: The Import Ban*, 1990).

Figure 48. Examples of a Citation of a Full Hearing.

Citing Unenacted Federal Bills and Resolutions

When you cite an unenacted federal bill or resolution in the text of your document, you must include the:

- name of the bill or resolution

- year in which the bill or resolution was introduced

Figure 49 shows two examples. The title of the hearing is italicized. When the citation is completely within the parentheses, as shown in the second example in Figure 49, only the initials are used and there is no space between the "H." and the "R." (for House of Representatives).

NOTE: *The correct abbreviation for a Senate Resolution or Bill when used in parentheses is "S."*

House of Representatives 504 (1986), introduced by Rep. Robert Badham, the Republican congressman from Newport Beach, California, sought to authorize establishment of a memorial in Washington, DC, or its environs to honor the Challenger astronauts.

or

In 1986, Congressman Robert Badham of Newport Beach, California, sought to pass a resolution authorizing the building of a memorial to the Challenger astronauts on federal land in the District of Columbia or its environs *(H.R. 504, 1986).*

Figure 49. Examples of a Citation of an Unenacted Federal Bill or Resolution.

Citing Enacted Federal Bills and Resolutions

When you cite an enacted federal bill or resolution in the text of your document, you must include the:

- name of the bill or resolution

- year in which the bill or resolution was passed

Bear in mind that enacted federal bills and resolutions are really laws, and, therefore, should be cited as statutes, if possible (see page 71).

Figure 50 shows two examples.

When the citation is completely within the parentheses, as shown in the second example in Figure 50, only the initial "S." is used.

NOTE: *The correct abbreviation for a Senate Resolution or Bill when used in parentheses is "S. Res." or "S. Bill." The correct abbreviation for a House Joint Resolution when used in parentheses is "H. J. Res."*

```
Lorem ipsum dolor sit amet, consectetuer adipiscing

elit, sed diam nonummy nibh euismod tin cidunt ut

laoreet dolore magna aliquam erat volutpat as stated

in Senate Bill 345 (1993).
```

or

```
Ut wisi enim ad minim veniam, quis nostrud exerci

tation ullamcorper suscipit lobortis nisl ut aliquip

ex ea commodo consequat (S. Res. 345, 1993).
```

Figure 50. Examples of a Citation of an Enacted Bill or Resolution.

Citing Federal Reports and Documents

When you cite a federal report or document in the text of your document, you must include the:

- number of the report or document

- year in which the report or document was issued

Figure 51 shows two examples.

When using the citation as part of your text, as shown in the first example in Figure 51, the words of the title are completely spelled out, with the exception of "Number," which is abbreviated as "No." The year of the Congress is included, then a hyphen, and the report number.

When the citation is completely within the parentheses, as shown in the second example in Figure 51, all the words of the title are abbreviated.

NOTE: *The correct abbreviation for a federal document, when used in parentheses, is "Doc"; i.e., (S. Doc. No. 1234, 1992).*

```
Lorem ipsum dolor sit amet, consectetuer adipiscing

elit, sed diam nonummy nibh euismod tin cidunt ut

laoreet dolore magna aliquam erat volutpat as stated

in Senate Report No. 104-123 (1993).
```

or

```
Ut wisi enim ad minim veniam, quis nostrud exerci

tation ullamcorper suscipit lobortis nisl ut aliquip

ex ea commodo consequat (S. Rep. No. 104-123, 1993).
```

Figure 51. Examples of a Citation of a Federal Report or Document.

Citing Administrative and Executive Materials

There are two types of administrative and executive materials:

- Federal rules and regulations

- Executive orders and advisory opinions

Citing a Federal Rule or Regulation

You'll find federal rules and regulations in both the *Code of Federal Regulations* and in the *Federal Register*. They are generally published first in the *Federal Register*, then codified in the *Code of Federal Regulations*.

When you cite a federal rule or regulation in the text of your document, you must include the:

- title of the rule or regulation

- year in which the rule or regulation was passed

Figure 52 shows two examples.

NOTE: *If the rule is contained in both the Code and the Register, cite the title from both sources. Put the title of the second citation in parentheses as a cross-reference.*

```
Lorem ipsum dolor sit amet, consectetuer adipiscing

elit, sed diam nonummy nibh euismod tin cidunt ut

laoreet dolore magna aliquam erat volutpat as stated

in the FTC Credit Practices Rule (1991).
```

or

```
Ut wisi enim ad minim veniam, quis nostrud exerci

ullamcorper suscipit lobortis nisl ut aliquip ex ea

commodo consequat (FTC Credit Practices Rule, 1991).
```

Figure 52. Examples of a Citation of a Federal Regulation.

Citing an Executive Order or Advisory Opinion

You'll find executive orders in Volume 3 of the *Code of Federal Regulations*. They may also be listed in the United States Code (U.S.C.).

When you cite an executive order or advisory opinion in the text of your document, you must include the:

- title (which includes the number) of the order or opinion

- year in which the rule or regulation was passed

If the executive order is contained in both the *Code of Federal Regulations* and the United States Code, cite the title from both sources. Put the title of the second citation in parentheses as a cross-reference.

Figure 53 shows two examples.

Lorem ipsum dolor sit amet, consectetuer adipiscing elit, sed diam nonummy nibh euismod tin cidunt ut laoreet dolore magna aliquam erat volutpat as stated in Executive Order No. 12,804, (1992).

or

Ut wisi enim ad minim veniam, quis nostrud exerci tation ullamcorper suscipit lobortis nisl ut aliquip ex ea commodo consequat (Executive Order No. 12,804, 1992).

Figure 53. Examples of a Citation of an Executive Order.

Chapter 6

Formatting the Frontis Material and Appendices

This chapter explains how to format the frontis material and the appendices of your report or article.

Formatting the Frontis Material

The frontis material of a report consists of the:

- title page

- executive summary (optional)

- table of contents

- list of figures

- list of tables

Formatting a Report or Article Title Page

Your instructor or professor may require you to include a title page on your report or article. Figure 54 shows a sample of a title page formatted according to APA requirements. It contains the following elements:

- Page header

- Running head*

- Title of report

- Author's name

- College or university name

Center your title page text, leaving lots of white space on either side. Note that all the elements are double-spaced.

Your instructor or professor may wish you to include other elements on the title page. For instance, you may be required to include the following:

- Name of class for which the report is being submitted

- Date

Check with him or her to find out these additional elements or whether you are supposed to use another format altogether.

---

* The running head is an abbreviated version of the title that is placed at the top of each page of the printed article; therefore, the running head is really meant for an article submitted to the APA Journal. Your instructor may not require you to include this since your report will not be published.

Attitudes Toward Telecommuting   1

Running Head: Attitudes Toward Telecommuting

Attitudes Toward Telecommuting

Among Managers and Employees at ABC Computer Co.

John Student

California State University - Fullerton

Figure 54. Example of a Report Title Page in APA Format.

Formatting an Executive Summary

If you are a business major, you may be required to include an executive summary in your document, even though APA format does not specifically have a format for this. The executive summary is short (approximately one page for reports) and includes all the pertinent information that any manager needs to understand exactly what you have studied, concluded, and recommended.

NOTE: *Do NOT include an executive summary unless your assignment requires it.*

The word "summary" means exactly that. You cannot summarize your report until you have written it. In other words, the Executive Summary is written last, but it is read first. Because the readers of the executive summary are generally non-technical, this document should be jargon-free.

The executive summary is double-spaced, with the words "Executive Summary" at the top per the example shown in Figure 55. It is generally placed right behind the title page and before the Table of Contents, if there is one, but check with your professor to find out if it should be located elsewhere.

NOTE: *The words "Executive Summary" should be in the same style as the first-level heading of your document.*

NOTE: *The example shown is page 2 because the report has a title page, which is page 1.*

Reorganization Plan   2

Executive Summary

Lorem ipsum dolor sit amet, consectetuer adipisci

elit, sed diam nonummy nibh eusmod tin cidunt ut loreet

dolore magna aliquam erat volutpat. Ut wisi ad minim

veniam, quis nostrud exerci tation ulcorper suscipit

lobortis nisl ut aliquip ex ea commodo consequat.

Duis atem vel eum iriure dolor in hendrerit in

putate velit esse molestie consequat, vel illum dolore

feugiat nulla facilisis at vero eros et accumsan et

odio dignissim qui blandit praesent luptatum zzril del

augue duis dolore te feugait nulla facilisi.

Nam liber tempor cum soluta nobis eleifend id

congue nihil imperdiet doming id quod mazim placerat

possim assum.

Lorem ipsum dolor sit amet, consectetuer adipisci

elit, sed diam nonummy nibh euismod tin cidunt ut loreet

dolore magna aliquam erat volutpat. The total cost to

carry out this plan is $24,000.00.

Figure 55. Example of the First Page of an Executive Summary.

Formatting a Table of Contents

While APA format does not require it, your instructor or professor may require you to include a Table of Contents, especially if your report is more than five pages. The Table of Contents is the roadmap by which your readers navigate through your document. The Table of Contents should contain all the headings in the body, worded exactly as they appear therein; therefore, the Table of Contents should not contain any headings that are not in the document and vice versa.

You can create the Table of Contents after your document is done. Many word processors have an automatic table of contents generator, which is easier, of course.

Figure 56 shows a sample first page of a Table of Contents for a report. Be sure to include all the appendices in the listing. Note that the title, Table of Contents, is not included in the Table of Contents itself, nor are the titles of any of the frontis material; rather, the Table of Contents starts with the body of the document.

NOTE: *The words "Table of Contents" should be in the same style as the first level heading of your document.*

Reorganization Plan   3

Table of Contents

Figure 56. Example of a Table of Contents.

Formatting a List of Figures

Strict APA guidelines require that you include your figure captions in the regular Table of Contents. Once again, this requirement is for publication purposes in the *APA Journal.* Your professor may wish a separate list of figures, however. This section shows you how to format such a list.

Just as the Table of Contents acts as a roadmap to guide your readers through the text of your document, the List of Figures is a roadmap to the drawings and pictures your document contains. In other words, it is the "table of contents" for your figures. Create a List of Figures if you have five or more figures in your document.

If your word processor has an automatic table of contents generator that will generate the List of Figures, use that. If you do not have too many figures, it may be just as easy to create the list by hand.

Figure 57 shows a sample List of Figures.

> ***NOTE:*** *The words "List of Figures" should be in the same style as the first-level heading of your document.*

Reorganization Plan   4

List of Figures

Figure 57. Example of a List of Figures.

Formatting a List of Tables

Strict APA guidelines require that you include your table captions in the regular Table of Contents. Once again, this requirement is for publication purposes in the *APA Journal*. Your professor may wish a separate list of tables, however. This section shows you how to format such a list.

Just as the Table of Contents acts as a roadmap to guide your readers through the text of your document and the List of Figures is a roadmap to the drawings and pictures, the List of Tables is a roadmap to the tables in your document. In other words, it is the "table of contents" for your tables. Create a List of Tables if you have three or more tables in your document.

If your word processor has an automatic table of contents generator that will generate the List of Tables, use that. If you do not have too many tables, it may be just as easy to create the list by hand.

Figure 58 shows a sample List of Tables.

NOTE: *The words "List of Tables" should be in the same style as the first-level heading of your document.*

Reorganization Plan   5

List of Tables

Figure 58. Example of a List of Tables.

Formatting the Appendices

If you have only one appendix, just call it "Appendix." If you have two or more appendices, however, call them Appendix A, Appendix B, and so on.

Strict APA guidelines require that you place the appendix letter and title on the first page of the material in the appendix. Your college or university, however, may wish you to create a separate title page for each one. Figure 59 shows an example of such a separate appendix title page. Include your information behind this title page.

Reorganization Factors   35

Appendix B

Reorganization Chart

for ABC Company

Figure 59. Example of an Appendix Title Page.

Chapter 7

Creating a Reference List

What is the difference between a bibliography and a reference list? Strictly speaking, a bibliography is a list of books ("biblio" is from the Greek word *biblion*, meaning book, and "-graphy" is the combining form meaning a writing; it is from the Greek word *graphein*, to write). In APA, a reference list includes references not only from books, but also from other sources, such as:

- journal articles

- magazine articles

- newsletter articles

- newspaper articles

- monographs

- abstracts

- company brochures

- personal interviews and correspondence

- encyclopedias or dictionaries

- government publications

- academic material

- raw data

- book, movie, and video reviews

- audio-visual media

- legal materials

- electronic media

Include in your reference list only the sources you actually used to research your report. This chapter shows you how to create all the types of references mentioned on page 93. Follow these rules when creating them:

- Place the word "References" at the top of the list.

- Create the list in alphabetical order by the author's last name.

- Follow the layout and punctuation exactly as shown in this chapter.

NOTE: *Many of the examples shown in this section are not real, but have been created for example purposes.*

For an example of a complete reference list, please see Appendix F.

Referencing Periodicals

This section shows you how to reference:

- journal articles

- magazine articles

- newsletters

- newspapers

- monographs

- abstracts

- periodicals published annually

- works discussed in secondary sources

Referencing Journal Articles

When you reference a journal article, you must reference both the article and the journal it is in. This section shows you how to reference a(n):

- journal article with one author

- journal article with two authors

- journal article with three to six authors

- journal article with seven or more authors

- journal article in press

- entire issue of a journal

- journal supplement

- non-English journal article with the title translated into English

- English translation of a journal article

Referencing a Journal Article With One Author

A reference for a journal article with one author appears as shown in Figure 60 and consists of the following elements:

- Author's last name

- Author's first initial, and middle initial, if available

- Year of journal issue

- Title of article

- Title of journal

- Volume (and issue) number, if available

- Page number(s) of article

To create this reference, follow these steps:

1. At the left margin, type the author's last name in full, followed by a comma and a space.

2. Type the author's first initial (*not* the full first name), followed by a period and a space, then the middle initial (if available), followed by a period and a space. If the author's middle name is not listed, just use the first initial.

Remember: *Never, never* use the full first name!

3. In parentheses, type the copyright year, followed by a period and a space.

4. Type the title of the article in plain type. Use an initial capital letter on the first word but use lower-case letters on the remaining words unless they are proper names. End with a period and a space.

5. Type the journal title. Use an initial capital letter on all main words and follow the title with a comma, a space, and the volume number, if available. Italicize the title and the volume number. (If the issue number is available, place it in parentheses and follow it with a comma, as shown).

6. Type a space and the page numbers, followed by a period.

    NOTE: Notice that the "pp." is not included in the page number shown in Figure 60. The "p." or "pp." is not used when the volume number is included.

7. If your reference continues to a second line, double-space the second line and indent it three spaces.

Follow this format exactly. See Appendix F for a complete list of references.

```
Matthews, Y. A. (1993). Electronic communication in

   large organizations. Technical Communication, 39(2),

   60-65.
```

Figure 60. Example of a Reference of a Journal Article With One Author.

Referencing a Journal Article With Two Authors

A reference for a journal article with two authors appears as shown in Figure 61 and consists of the following elements:

- Both authors' last names

- Both authors' first initials

- Year of journal issue

- Title of article

- Title of journal

- Volume (and issue) number, if available

- Page number(s) of article

To create this reference, follow these steps:

1. At the left margin, type the first author's last name in full, followed by a comma and a space.

2. Type the first author's first initial (*not* the full first name), followed by a period, a comma, and a space.

Remember: *Never, never* use the full first name!

3. Type an ampersand (&) and a space.

4. Type the second author's last name, followed by a comma and a space.

5. Type the second author's first initial, followed by a period and a space.

6. In parentheses, type the copyright year, followed by a period and a space.

7. Type the title of the article in plain type. Use an initial capital letter on the first word but use lower-case letters on the remaining words unless they are proper names. End the title with a period and a space.

8. Type the journal title. Use an initial capital letter on all main words and follow the title with a comma, a space, and the volume number, if available. Italicize the title and the volume number. If the issue number is available, place it in parentheses in plain type and follow it with a comma and a space, as shown in Figure 61.

9.   Type the page numbers, followed by a period.

> **NOTE:** *Notice that the "pp." is not included in the page number shown in Figure 61. The "p." or "pp." is not used when the volume number is included.*

10.   If your reference continues to a second line, double-space the second line and indent it three spaces.

Follow this format exactly. See Appendix F for a complete list of references.

```
Matthews, Y., & Jones, T. (1993). Electronic

    communication in large organizations. Technical

    Communication, 39(2), 60-65.
```

Figure 61. Example of a Reference of a Journal Article With Two Authors.

Referencing a Journal Article With Three to Six Authors

A reference for a journal article with three to six authors appears as shown in Figure 62 and consists of the following elements:

- Authors' last names

- Authors' first initials and middle initials, if available

- Year of journal issue

- Title of article

- Title of journal

- Volume (and issue) number, if available

- Page number(s) of article

To create this reference, follow these steps:

1. At the left margin, type the first author's last name in full, followed by a comma and a space.

2. Type the first author's first initial (*not* the full first name), followed by a period and a space, then the middle initial, if available, a period, a comma, and a space.

Remember: *Never, never* use the full first name!

3. Type the second author's last name in full, followed by a comma and a space.

4. Repeat Step 3 for all authors except the last.

5. After the next-to-the-last author's middle initial (or first initial, if the middle initial is not available), type an ampersand (&) and a space.

6. Type the last author's last name, followed by a comma and a space.

7. Type the last author's first initial, followed by a period and a space, then the middle initial, if available, followed by a period and a space.

8. In parentheses, type the copyright year, followed by a period and a space.

9. Type the title of the article in plain type. Use an initial capital letter on the first word but use lower-case letters on the remaining words unless they are proper names. End the title with a period and a space.

10. Type the journal title. Use an initial capital letter on all main words and follow the title with a comma, a space, and the volume number, if available. Italicize the title and the volume number. (If the issue number is available, place it in parentheses and follow it with a comma, as shown in Figure 62.)

11. Type a space and the page numbers, followed by a period.

    NOTE: *Notice that the "pp." is not included in the page number shown in Figure 62. The "p." or "pp." is not used when the volume number is included.*

12. If your reference continues to a second line, double-space the second line and indent it three spaces.

Follow this format exactly. See Appendix F for a complete list of references.

```
Ridgeway, L. S., Grice, R. A., & Gould, E. (1992). I'm

   ok, you're only a user. Technical Communication, 39

(1), 38-49.
```

Figure 62. Example of a Reference of a Journal Article With Three to Six Authors.

Referencing a Journal Article With Seven or More Authors

A reference for a journal article with seven or more authors appears as shown in Figure 63 and consists of the following elements:

- Authors' last names

- First and second authors' first initials and middle initials, if available

- Third through last authors' first initials

- Year of journal issue

- Title of article

- Title of journal

- Volume (and issue) number, if available

- Page number(s) of article

To create this reference, follow these steps:

1. At the left margin, type the first author's last name in full, followed by a comma and a space.

2. Type the first author's first initial (*not* the full first name), followed by a period and a space, then the middle initial, if available, a period, a comma, and a space.

Remember: *Never, never* use the full first name!

3. Type the second author's last name in full, followed by a comma and a space.

4. Type the second author's first initial (*not* the full first name), followed by a period and a space, then the middle initial, if available, a period, a comma, and a space.

5. Type the third author's last name in full, followed by a comma and a space.

6. Type the third author's first initial only (*not* the full first name), followed by followed by a period and a space.

7. Repeat Steps 5 and 6 for all remaining authors except the last.

8. Type an ampersand (&) and a space.

9. Type the last author's last name, followed by a comma and a space.

10. Type the last author's first initial, followed by a period and a space.

11. In parentheses, type the copyright year, followed by a period and a space.

12. Type the title of the article in plain type. Use an initial capital letter on the first word but use lower-case letters on the remaining words unless they are proper names. End with a period and a space.

13. Type the journal title. Use an initial capital letter on all main words and follow the title with a comma, a space, and the volume number, if available. Italicize the title and the volume number. If the issue number is available, place it in parentheses and follow it with a comma, as shown in Figure 63.

14. Type a space and the page numbers, followed by a period.

> **NOTE:** *Notice that the "pp." is not included in the page number shown in Figure 63. The "p." or "pp." is not used when the volume number is included.*

15. If your reference continues to a second line, double-space the second line and indent it three spaces.

Follow this format exactly. See Appendix F for a complete list of references.

```
Ridgeway, L. S., Grice, R. A., Jones, T., Cruz, A.,

    Washington, K., & Gould, E. (1992).  I'm ok; You're

only a user. Technical Communication, 39(1), 38-49.
```

Figure 63. Example of a Reference of a Journal Article With Seven or More Authors.

Referencing a Journal Article In Press

You may reference an article that has been accepted for publication, but the journal has not yet been published. This article is then "in press." Let's say it has one author. A reference for a journal article in press with one author appears as shown in Figure 64 and consists of the following elements:

- Author's last name

- Author's first initial, and middle initial, if available

- Year of journal issue

- Title of article

- Title of journal

- Volume (and issue) number, if available

- Page number(s) of article

To create this reference, follow these steps:

1. At the left margin, type the author's last name in full, followed by a comma and a space.

2. Type the author's first initial (*not* the full first name), followed by a period and a space, then the middle initial (if available), followed by a period and a space. If the author's middle name is not listed, just use the first initial.

Remember: *Never, never* use the full first name!

3. In parentheses, type the copyright year, followed by a period and a space.

4. Type the title of the article in plain type. Use an initial capital letter on the first word but use lower-case letters on the remaining words unless they are proper names. End the title with a period and a space.

5. Type the journal title. Use an initial capital letter on all main words and follow the title with a comma, a space, and the volume number, if available. Italicize the title and the volume number. If the issue number is available, place it in parentheses and follow it with a comma, as shown in Figure 64.

6. Type a space and the page numbers, followed by a period.

> **NOTE:** *Notice that the "pp." is not included in the page number shown in Figure 64. The "p." or "pp." is not used when the volume number is included.*

7. If your reference continues to a second line, double-space the second line and indent it three spaces.

Follow this format exactly. See Appendix F for a complete list of references.

> **NOTE:** *If the article has more than one author, follow the rules for that number of authors.*

```
Fye, W. B. (1991). The origin of the full-time faculty

    system. Education Today, 265(1), 38-49.
```

Figure 64. Example of a Reference of a Journal Article in Press.

NOTE: *In the text, cite the article as follows:*

```
(Fye, in press)
```

or

```
Fye (in press) states....
```

Referencing an Entire Issue of a Journal

A reference for an entire issue of a journal appears as shown in Figure 65 and consists of the following elements:

- Editor's last name

- Editor's first initial, and middle initial, if available

- Abbreviation "Ed."

- Year of journal issue

- Title of journal issue

- Words "Special issue"

- Title of journal

- Volume (and issue) number, if available

To create this reference, follow these steps:

1. At the left margin, type the editor's last name in full, followed by a comma and a space.

2. Type the editor's first initial, followed by a period and a space, then the middle initial (if available), followed by a period and a space. If the editor's middle name is not listed, just use the first initial.

Remember: *Never, never* use the full first name!

3. Type the abbreviation "Ed." in parentheses, followed by a period and a space.

4. In parentheses, type the copyright year, followed by a period and a space.

5. Type the special issue title in plain type. Use an initial capital letter on the first word but use initial lower-case letters on the remaining words unless they are proper names. Follow this with a period and a space.

6. In brackets, type "Special issue," followed by a period and a space. Capitalize the "S" on "special."

7. Type the journal title. Use an initial capital letter on all main words and follow the title with a comma, a space, and the volume number, if available. Italicize the title and the volume number. If the issue number is available, place it in parentheses. Follow the information with a period.

8. If your reference continues to a second line, double-space the second line and indent it three spaces.

Follow this format exactly. See Appendix F for a complete list of references.

Shelton, S. M. (Ed.). (1991). Visual communication

[Special issue]. *Technical Communication, 40*(4).

Figure 65. Example of a Reference of an Entire Issue of a Journal.

Referencing a Journal Supplement

A reference for a journal supplement appears as shown in Figure 66 and consists of the following elements:

- Author's/editor's last name

- Author's/editor's first initial, and middle initial, if available

- Year of journal issue

- Title of journal

- Title of journal

- Volume (and issue) number, if available

- Abbreviation "Suppl." and the supplement number

- Page numbers

To create this reference, follow these steps:

1. At the left margin, type the author's/editor's last name in full, followed by a comma and a space.

2. Type the author's/editor's first initial, followed by a period and a space, then the middle initial (if available), followed by a period, a comma, and a space. If the author's/editor's middle name is not listed, just use the first initial.

   If the supplement has an editor rather than an author, type the abbreviation "Ed." in parentheses (as shown in Figure 66), followed by a period and a space.

Remember: *Never, never use the full first name!*

3. In parentheses, type the copyright year, followed by a period and a space.

4. In italics, type the title of the supplement. Use an initial capital letter on the first word but use initial lower-case letters on the remaining words unless they are proper names. Type a period and a space.

5. In italics, type the journal title. Use an initial capital letter on all main words and follow the title with a comma, a space, and the volume number, if available. Italicize the title and the volume number.

6. Immediately following the volume number, in parentheses, put the abbreviation "Suppl.," followed by a space, and then the supplement number.

7. After the closing parenthesis, type a space and then the page numbers (do not use "p." or "pp.").

8. If your reference continues to a second line, double-space the second line and indent it three spaces.

Follow this format exactly. See Appendix F for a complete list of references.

```
Shelton, S. M. (Ed.). (1991). Visual communication.

   Technical Communication, 40(Suppl. 4), 18-24.
```

Figure 66. Example of a Reference of a Journal Supplement.

Referencing a Non-English Journal Article With the Title Translated into English

A reference for a non-English journal article with the title translated into English appears as shown in Figure 67 and consists of the following elements:

- Author's last name

- Author's first initial, and middle initial, if available

- Copyright year of journal

- Original title of article

- Title of article in English

- Title of journal

- Volume (and issue) number, if available

- Page numbers

To create this reference, follow these steps:

1. At the left margin, type the author's last name in full, followed by a comma.

2. Type the author's first initial, followed by a period and a space, then the middle initial (if available), followed by a period, a comma, and a space. If the author's middle name is not listed, just use the first initial.

Remember: *Never, never* use the full first name!

3. In parentheses, type the copyright year, followed by a period and a space.

4. In plain type, type the original title of the article. Use an initial capital letter on the first word but use lower-case letters on the remaining words, unless they are proper names. (In German, all nouns are capitalized; therefore, they are capitalized in Figure 69). Include any diacritical marks. After the title, type a space.

5. In brackets, type the English title of the article, followed by a period and a space. Use an initial capital letter on the first word but use lower-case letters on the remaining words, unless they are proper names.

6. Type the journal title. Use an initial capital letter on all main words and follow the title with a comma, a space, and the volume number, if available. Italicize the title, the volume number, and the commas. If the issue number is available, place it in parentheses and follow it with a comma and a space (not shown in Figure 67.)

7. Type the page numbers, followed by a period.

NOTE: *Notice that the "pp." is not included in the page number shown in Figure 67. The "p." or "pp." is not used when the volume number is included.*

8. If your reference continues to a second line, double-space the second line and indent it three spaces.

Follow this format exactly. See Appendix F for a complete list of references.

```
Zajonc, R. B. (1989). Bischofs gefühlvolle Verwirrunggen

   über die Gefühle [Bischof's emotional flare over the

   emotions]. Psychologische Rundschau, 40, 218-211.
```

Figure 67. Example of a Reference of a Non-English Journal Article With the Title Translated into English.

Referencing an English Translation of a Journal Article

A reference for an English translation of a journal article appears as shown in Figure 68 and consists of the following elements:

- Author's last name

- Author's first initial

- Copyright year of journal

- English title of article

- Title of journal

- Volume (and issue) number, if available

- Page numbers

To create this reference, follow these steps:

1. At the left margin, type the author's last name in full, followed by a comma and a space.

2. Type the author's first initial, followed by a period and a space.

Remember: *Never, never* use the full first name!

3. In parentheses, type the copyright year, followed by a period and a space.

4. In plain type, type the title of the article, followed by a period and a space. Use an initial capital letter on the first word but use lower-case letters on the remaining words unless they are proper names.

5. Type the journal title. Use an initial capital letter on all main words and follow the title with a comma, a space, and the volume number, if available. Italicize the title and the volume number. If the issue number is available, place it in parentheses and follow it with a comma.

6. Type a space and the page numbers, followed by a period.

NOTE: *Notice that the "pp." is not included in the page number shown in Figure 68. The "p." or "pp." is not used when the volume number is included.*

7.   Type the page numbers.

8.   If your reference continues to a second line, double-space the second line and indent it three spaces.

Follow this format exactly. See Appendix F for a complete list of references.

```
Zajonc, R. (1989). Bischof's emotional flare over the

    emotions. Psychologische Rundschau, 40, 218-211.
```

Figure 68. Example of a Reference of an English Translation of a Journal Article.

Referencing Magazine Articles

This section shows you how to reference a:

- magazine article with an author

- magazine article with no author

Referencing a Magazine Article With An Author

When you reference a magazine article with an author, you must reference both the article and the magazine it is in. A reference for a magazine article with an author appears as shown in Figure 69 and consists of the following elements:

- Author's last name

- Author's first initial, and middle initial, if available

- Year, month, (and day, if applicable) of magazine issue

- Title of article

- Title of magazine

- Volume number, if available

- Page number(s) of article

To create this reference, follow these steps:

1. At the left margin, type the author's last name in full, followed by a comma and a space.

2. Type the author's first initial (*not* the full first name), followed by a period and a space, then the middle initial (if available), followed by a period and a space. If the author's middle name is not listed, just use the first initial.

   Remember: Never, never use the full first name!

3. In parentheses, type the copyright year, followed by a comma, a space, the month of publication (and the day, too, if applicable (e.g., June 15)), a period, and a space.

4. In plain type, type the title of the article. Use an initial capital letter on the first word but use lower-case letters on the remaining words unless they are proper names. End the title with a period and a space.

5. Type the magazine title. Use an initial capital letter on all main words and follow the title with a comma, a space, and the volume number, if available, and another comma. Italicize the title, the volume number, and the commas.

6. Type a space and the page numbers, followed by a period.

NOTE: *Notice that the "pp." is not included in the page number shown in Figure 69. The "p." or "pp." is not used when the volume number is included; therefore, use these initials only when the volume number is not included.*

7. If your reference continues to a second line, double-space the second line and indent it three spaces.

Follow this format exactly. See Appendix F for a complete list of references.

```
Morrison, H. A. (1992, December). The paperless office.

   Business Talk, 115, 70-76.
```

Figure 69. Example of a Reference of a Magazine Article With an Author.

Referencing a Magazine Article With No Author

Many articles are "staff-written"; that is, they are written by someone on the magazine's staff and do not exhibit a byline.

When you reference a magazine article with no author, you must reference both the article and the magazine. An example appears as shown in Figure 70 and consists of the following elements:

- Title of magazine

- Title of article

- Month (and day, if applicable) and year of magazine issue

- Page number(s) of article

To create this reference, follow these steps:

1. At the left margin, type the magazine title. Use an initial capital letter on all main words and follow the title a period and a space. Italicize the title and the period.

2. In parentheses, type the copyright year, followed by a comma, a space, and the month of publication (the day, too, if applicable; i.e., June 15), and then a period and a space.

3. Type the article title in plain type. Use an initial capital letter on the first word but lower-case letters on the remaining words unless they are proper names. End the title with a period and a space.

4. Type "P." (or "Pp." if there is a range of pages, as shown in Figure 70) and the page number(s), followed by a period. The first "p" is capitalized because it begins the sentence.

5. If your reference continues to a second line, double-space the second line and indent it three spaces.

Follow this format exactly. See Appendix F for a complete list of references.

```
Business Talk. (1992, December). Time management

     tips. Pp. 70-76.
```

Figure 70. Example of a Reference of a Magazine Article With No Author.

Referencing Newsletter Articles

Referencing a Newsletter Article With an Author

When you reference a newsletter article with an author, you must reference both the article and the newsletter it is in. A reference for a newsletter article with an author appears as shown in Figure 71 and consists of the following elements:

- Author's last name

- Author's first initial, and middle initial, if available

- Year, month, (and day, if applicable) (or season) of newletter issue

- Title of article

- Title of newsletter

- Volume number, if available

- Page number(s) of article

To create this reference, follow these steps:

1. At the left margin, type the author's last name in full, followed by a comma and a space.

2. Type the author's first initial (*not* the full first name), followed by a period and a space, then the middle initial (if available), followed by a period and a space. If the author's middle name is not listed, just use the first initial.

Remember: *Never, never* use the full first name!

3. In parentheses, type the copyright year, followed by a comma, a space, the month of publication (and the day, too, if applicable (i.e., June 15)) or the season, and then a period and a space.

4. Type the title of the article in plain type. Use an initial capital letter on the first word but use lower-case letters on the remaining words unless they are proper names. End the title with a period and a space. (If the title ends with a question mark, as shown in Figure 71, or an exclamation point, do not use a period.)

5. Type the newsletter title. Use an initial capital letter on all main words and follow the title with a comma, a space, and the volume number, if available, and another comma. Italicize the title, the volume number, and the commas.

6. Type a space and the page numbers, followed by a period.

NOTE: *Notice that the "pp." is not included in the page number shown in Figure 71. The "p." or "pp." is not used when the volume number is included.*

7. If your reference continues to a second line, double-space the second line and indent it three spaces.

Follow this format exactly. See Appendix F for a complete list of references.

```
Jones, L. B. (1994, Spring). Employees or independent

contractors?  The Small Business Newsletter, 24,

22-24.
```

Figure 71. Example of a Reference of a Newsletter Article With an Author.

Referencing a Newsletter Article With No Author

Many articles are "staff-written"; that is, they are written by someone on the newsletter's staff and do not exhibit a byline. When you reference a newsletter article with no author, you must reference both the article and the newsletter. An example appears as shown in Figure 72 and consists of the following elements:

- Title of article

- Year, month, (and day, if applicable) of issue

- Title of newsletter

- Volume number

- Page number(s) of article

To create this reference, follow these steps:

1. At the left margin, type the article title. Use an initial capital letter on the first word but lower-case letters on the remaining words unless they are proper names. End with a period and a space.

2. In parentheses, type the copyright year, followed by a comma, a space, the month of publication (the day, too, if applicable; i.e., June 15), and then a period and a space.

3. Type the newsletter title, followed by a comma, a space, the volume number, if available, and another comma. Italicize the title, the volume number, and the commas.

4. Type the page numbers, followed by a period.

5. If your reference continues to a second line, double-space the second line and indent it three spaces.

Follow this format exactly. See Appendix F for a complete list of references.

```
The IRS' Section 1706 tax laws. (1992, May). The

    Consultant's News, 14, 24-26.
```

Figure 72. Example of a Reference of a Newsletter Article With No Author.

Referencing Newspaper Articles

This section shows you how to reference a:

- newspaper article with an author

- newspaper article with no author

- letter to the editor

Referencing a Newspaper Article With an Author

Reference a newspaper article with an author lke a magazine article with an author. Just put the newspaper's name where the magazine title goes. A reference for a newspaper article appears as shown in Figure 73 and consists of the following elements:

- Author's last name

- Author's first initial, and middle initial, if available

- Title of article

- Title of newspaper

- Month, day, and year of newspaper issue

- Page number(s) of article

To create this reference, follow these steps:

1. At the left margin, type the author's last name in full, followed by a comma and a space.

2. Type the author's first initial (*not* the full first name), followed by a period and a space, then the middle initial (if available), followed by a period and a space. If the author's middle name is not listed, just use the first initial.

    Remember: *Never, never* use the full first name!

3. In parentheses, type the copyright year, followed by a comma, a space, the month of publication (the day, too, if applicable; i.e., June 15), and then a period and a space.

4. Type the title of the article in plain type. Use an initial capital letter on the first word but use lower-case letters on all the remaining words unless they are proper names. End the title with a period and a space. (If the title ends with a question mark, as shown in Figure 73, or an exclamation point, do not use a period.)

5. In italics, type the newspaper title. Use initial capital letters on all words of the title and follow it with a comma and a space.

6. Type "p." (or "pp." for a range of pages) and the section letter and page number(s), followed by a period.

    Type discontinous pages in the following format: pp. B1, B3.

7. If your reference continues to a second line, double-space the second line and indent it three spaces.

Follow this format exactly. See Appendix F for a complete list of references.

```
Jones, J. T. (1993, December 10). Is an upturn in

    California's economy still years away? Los Angeles

    Times, p. B24.
```

Figure 73. Example of a Reference of a Newspaper Article With an Author.

Referencing a Newspaper Article With No Author

Just as with magazines, some newspaper articles are staff-written and have no byline credit. A reference for a newspaper article with no author appears as shown in Figure 74 and consists of the following elements:

- Title of article

- Year, month, and day of newspaper issue

- Title of newspaper

- Page number(s) of article

To create this reference, follow these steps:

1. At the left margin, type the title of the article in plain type. Use an initial capital letter on the first word but use lower-case letters on all the remaining words unless they are proper names unless they are proper names. End the title with a period and a space. (If the title ends with a question mark, as shown in Figure 74, or an exclamation point, do not use a period.)

2. In parentheses, type the copyright year, followed by a comma, a space, the month of publication (and the day, too, if applicable (i.e., June 15)), and then a period and a space.

3. Type the newspaper title, then italicize it. Use initial capital letters on all main words of the title and follow it with a comma and a space.

4. Type "p." (or "pp." for a range of pages) and the page number(s), followed by a period. Type discontinuous pages in the following format: B1, B3.

5. If your reference continues to a second line, double-space the second line and indent it three spaces.

Follow this format exactly. See Appendix F for a complete list of references.

Is an upturn in California's economy still years away?

(1993, December 10). *Los Angeles Times*, p. B-24.

Figure 74. Example of a Reference of a Newspaper Article With No Author.

Referencing a Letter to the Editor

Letters to the editor are letters subscribers write to the newspaper expressing their opinions about stories the newspaper has printed. They usually appear on the opinion or editorial (Op/Ed) page. A reference for a letter to the editor appears as shown in Figure 75 and consists of the following elements:

- Author's last name

- Author's first initial, and middle initial, if available

- Title of article

- Phrase "Letter to the editor"

- Title of newspaper

- Month, day, and year of newspaper issue

- Page number(s) of article

To create this reference, follow these steps:

1. At the left margin, type the author's last name in full, followed by a comma and a space.

2. Type the author's first initial (*not* the full first name), followed by a period and a space, then the middle initial (if available), followed by a period and a space. If the author's middle name is not listed, just use the first initial.

Remember: *Never, never* use the full first name!

3. In parentheses, type the copyright year, followed by the month of publication (the day, too, if applicable; i.e., June 15), and then a period and a space.

4. Type the title of the article in plain type. Use an initial capital letter on the first word but use lower-case letters on all the remaining words unless they are proper names. Follow the title with a space.

5. In brackets, type the phrase "Letter to the editor." Capitalize the "L" on "Letter," and type the rest of the words in lower-case letters. End with a period and a space.

6. Type the newspaper title, then italicize it. Capitalize all words of the title and follow it with a comma and a space.

7. Type "p." (or "pp." for a range of pages) and the section letter and page number(s), followed by a period.

    Type discontinous pages in the following format: pp. B1, B3.

8. If your reference continues to a second line, double-space the second line and indent it three spaces.

Follow this format exactly. See Appendix F for a complete list of references.

```
Jones, J. T. (1993, December 10). Welfare or

    workfare [Letter to the editor]. Los Angeles

    Times, p. B-24.
```

Figure 75. Example of a Reference of a Letter to the Editor.

Referencing Monographs

This section shows you how to reference a:

- monograph with an issue number and serial (or whole) number

- monograph bound separately as a supplement to a journal

- monograph bound into a journal

Referencing a Monograph With an Issue Number and Serial (or Whole) Number

A reference for a monograph with an issue number and serial (or whole) number is shown in Figure 76 and consists of the following elements:

- Author's last name

- Author's first initial, and middle initial, if available

- Copyright year

- Title of monograph

- Title of monograph series

- Volume number

- Issue number

- Serial (or whole) number

To create this reference, follow these steps:

1. At the left margin, type the author's last name in full, followed by a comma and a space.

2. Type the author's first initial (*not* the full first name), followed by a period and a space, then the middle initial (if available), followed by a period and a space. If the author's middle name is not listed, just use the first initial.

Remember: *Never, never* use the full first name!

3. In parentheses, type the copyright year, followed by a period and a space.

4. Type the title of the monograph, followed by a period and a space. Use an initial capital letter on the first word but use lower-case letters on all the remaining words unless they are proper names.

5. Type the title of the monograph series, followed by a comma, a space, and the volume number. Italicize all of these elements. Use initial capital letters on all main words of the title.

6. Immediately after the volume number, in parentheses, type the issue number, a comma, a space, the words "Serial No." (or the words "Whole No.," if applicable), a period, and a space.

7. Type the serial (or whole) number itself, followed by a closing parenthesis and a period.

8. If your reference continues to a second line, double-space the second line and indent it three spaces.

Follow this format exactly. See Appendix F for a complete list of references.

Smith, H. N. (1992). Five prehistoric sites in Orange

County, California. *Monographs of the South County*

Museum, 18(2, Serial No. 134).

Figure 76. Example of a Reference of a Monograph With an Issue Number and Serial (or Whole) Number.

Referencing a Monograph Bound Separately as a Supplement to a Journal

A reference for a monograph bound separately as a supplement to a journal is shown in Figure 77 and consists of the following elements:

- Author's last name

- Author's first initial, and middle initial, if available

- Copyright year

- Title of monograph

- Title of monograph series

- Volume number

- Issue number

- Abbreviation "Suppl." or "Pt."

- Supplement or part number

To create this reference, follow these steps:

1. At the left margin, type the author's last name in full, followed by a comma and a space.

2. Type the author's first initial (*not* the full first name), followed by a period and a space, then the middle initial (if available), followed by a period and a space. If the author's middle name is not listed, just use the first initial.

   Remember: *Never, never* use the full first name!

3. In parentheses, type the copyright year, followed by a period and a space.

4. Type the title of the monograph, followed by a period and a space. Use an initial capital letter on the first word but use lower-case letters on all the remaining words unless they are proper names.

5. Type the title of the monograph series, followed by a comma, a space, the volume number. Italicize these elements. Use initial capital letters on all main words of the title.

6. Immediately after the volume number, in parentheses, type the issue number, a comma, a space, and the abbreviation "Pt." for "part" (or "Suppl.," if it is a supplement number), a space, and then the part number (or supplement number) itself. End with a period.

7. If your reference continues to a second line, double-space the second line and indent it three spaces.

Follow this format exactly. See Appendix F for a complete list of references.

Smith, H. N. (1992). Five prehistoric sites in Orange

   County, California. *Monographs of the South County*

   Museum, 18(2, Pt. 3).

Figure 77. Example of a Reference of a Monograph Bound Separately as a Supplement to a Journal.

Referencing a Monograph Bound into a Journal

A reference for a monograph bound into a journal is shown in Figure 78 and consists of the following elements:

- Author's last name

- Author's first initial, and middle initial, if available

- Copyright year

- Title of monograph

- The word "Monograph"

- Journal title

- Volume number

- Page numbers

To create this reference, follow these steps:

1. At the left margin, type the author's last name in full, followed by a comma and a space.

2. Type the author's first initial (*not* the full first name), followed by a period and a space, then the middle initial (if available), followed by a period and a space. If the author's middle name is not listed, just use the first initial.

   Remember: *Never, never* use the full first name!

3. In parentheses, type the copyright year, followed by a period and a space.

4. Type the title of the monograph, followed by a space. Use an initial capital letter on the first word but use lower-case letters on all the remaining words unless they are proper names.

5. In brackets, type the word "Monograph," followed by a period and a space.

6. Type the title of the journal, followed by a comma, a space, and the volume number. Italicize all of these elements. Use initial capital letters on all main words of the title.

7. Type a space, and then the page numbers and a period. Figure 78 shows continuous numbers; that is, the monograph appears in one continuous section of the journal rather than starting in one section and being continued in another.

NOTE: *Notice that the "pp." is not included in the page number shown in Figure 78. The "p." or "pp." is not used when the volume number is included.*

8. If your reference continues to a second line, double-space the second line and indent it three spaces.

Follow this format exactly. See Appendix F for a complete list of references.

Smith, H. N. (1992). Five prehistoric sites in Orange

County, California [Monograph]. *Journal of the*

Southwest Archeological Association, 18, 88-125.

Figure 78. Example of a Reference of a Monograph Bound into a Journal with Continuous Pagination.

Referencing Abstracts

This section shows you how to reference an:

- abstract from an original source

- abstract from a secondary source

Referencing an Abstract as an Original Source

Sometimes, you will find an abstract that you want to reference as an original source. A reference for an abstract as an original source is shown in Figure 79 and consists of the following elements:

- Author's last name

- Author's first initial, and middle initial, if available

- Copyright year

- Title of paper or article abstract is from

- Journal title

- Volume number

- Page number(s)

To create this reference, follow these steps:

1. At the left margin, type the author's last name in full, followed by a comma and a space.

2. Type the author's first initial (*not* the full first name), followed by a period and a space, then the middle initial (if available), followed by a period and a space. If the author's middle name is not listed, just use the first initial.

Remember: Never, never use the full first name!

3. In parentheses, type the copyright year, followed by a period and a space.

4. Type the title of the paper or article the abstract is from, followed by a period and a space. Use an initial capital letter on the first word but use lower-case letters on all the remaining words unless they are proper names.

NOTE: *If the title of the journal or periodical itself does not include the word "abstracts," type "Abstract" in brackets between the last word of the title and the period, as shown in the second example in Figure 79.*

5. Type the title of the journal, followed by a comma, a space, and the volume number. Use initial capital letters on all main words of the title. Italicize these elements.

6. Type a space, and then the page number and a period.

NOTE: *Notice that the "p." is not included in the page number shown in Figure 79. The "p." or "pp." is not used when the volume number is included.*

7. If your reference continues to a second line, double-space the second line and indent it three spaces.

Follow this format exactly. See Appendix F for a complete list of references.

Smith, H. N. (1992). Five prehistoric sites in Orange

County, California. *Abstracts of the Journal of*

the Southwest Archeological Association, 18, 250.

Smith, H. N. (1992). Five prehistoric sites in Orange

County, California [Abstract]. *Southwest*

Archeological Association, 18, 250.

Figure 79. Examples of a Reference of an Abstract as an Original Source.

Referencing an Abstract From a Secondary Source

Sometimes, you will find an abstract that you want to reference that is referenced in someone else's work. This is called an abstract from a secondary source. A reference for an abstract from a secondary source is shown in Figure 80 and consists of the following elements:

- Author's last name

- Author's first initial, and middle initial, if available

- Copyright year

- Title of paper or article abstract is from

- Journal title

- Volume number

- Page number(s)

- Words "Abstract obtained from"

- Secondary source information

To create this reference, follow these steps:

1. At the left margin, type the author's last name in full, followed by a comma and a space.

2. Type the author's first initial (*not* the full first name), followed by a period and a space, then the middle initial (if available), followed by a period and a space. If the author's middle name is not listed, just use the first initial.

Remember: *Never, never* use the full first name!

3. In parentheses, type the copyright year of the *original* abstract, followed by a period and a space.

4. Type the title of the paper or article the abstract is from, followed by a period and a space. Use an initial capital letter on the first word but use lower-case letters on all the remaining words unless they are proper names.

5. Type the title of the journal, followed by a comma, a space, the volume number, and another comma. Italicize all of these. Use initial capital letters on all main words of the title.

6. Type a space, and then the page number(s), a period, and a space.

   NOTE: *Notice that the "p." is not included in the page number shown in Figure 80. The "p." or "pp." is not used when the volume number is included.*

7. Type the words "Abstract obtained from" and a space.

8. Cite the secondary source information, including the source, followed by a colon, and the title of the periodical, followed by a comma and a space. Italicize these elements.

9. Type the year the periodical was published, a comma, a space, the volume number, another space, and the abstract no.

10. If your reference continues to a second line, double-space the second line and indent it three spaces.

    NOTE: *If the date of the secondary source is different from the date of the original source, include both dates in the your text citation (in the body of your paper). Cite the original source date first, type a slash, Type the secondary source date (e.g., (1992/1993)).*

Follow this format exactly. See Appendix F for a complete list of references.

NOTE: *If the title of the series changes with each issue, reference the series as a book or chapter in an edited book.*

```
Smith, H. N. (1998). Five prehistoric sites in Orange

   County, California. Journal of the Southwest

   Archeological Association, 18, 12-19. Abstract

   obtained from ArcSCAN: The American Southwest

   Monthly, 1999, 7, Abstract No. 151.
```

Figure 80. Example of a Reference of an Abstract From a Secondary Source.

Referencing a Periodical Published Annually

A reference for a periodical published annually is shown in Figure 81 and consists of the following elements:

- Author's last name

- Author's first initial, and middle initial, if available

- Copyright year

- Title of issue

- Periodical title

- Volume number

- Page number(s)

To create this reference, follow these steps:

1. At the left margin, type the author's last name in full, followed by a comma.

2. Type the author's first initial (*not* the full first name), followed by a period and a space, then the middle initial (if available), followed by a period, a comma, and a space. If the author's middle name is not listed, just use the first initial.

Remember: *Never, never* use the full first name!

3. In parentheses, type the copyright year, followed by a period and a space.

4. Type the title of the issue, followed by a period and a space. Use an initial capital letter on the first word but use lower-case letters on all the remaining words unless they are proper names.

5. Type the title of the periodical, followed by a comma, a space, the volume number, and another comma. Italicize these elements. Use initial capital letters on all main words of the title.

6. Type a space, and then the page number(s) and a period.

NOTE: *Notice that the "p." is not included in the page number shown in Figure 81. The "p." or "pp." is not used when the volume number is included.*

7. If your reference continues to a second line, double-space the second line and indent it three spaces.

Follow this format exactly. See Appendix F for a complete list of references.

Smith, H. N. (1992). Trends in human resources. *Annual*

   Review of Business, 18, 12-19.

Figure 81. Example of a Reference of a Periodical Published Annually.

Referencing a Work Discussed in a Secondary Source

Sometimes you will want to reference an article or book that is cited in someone else's work. In the references, list the information of the secondary source. Follow the rules for the type of reference it is; i.e., a book, journal article, newspaper article, etc.

Referencing Books

This section shows you how to reference a book with:

- one author

- two authors

- multiple authors

- a group author

- an editor

- an author and editor

- no author or editor

- a subtitle

- an article or chapter in a book

- an article or chapter in an edited book

When you reference books, you must include the city where the publisher is located. If the city does not appear in Table 15, you must include the two-letter state or territory code (see Table 14, page 54) or the country name.

Table 15. Cities Not Needing State or Territory Code or Country Name in the Reference List.

AMERICAN CITIES		FOREIGN CITIES	
Baltimore	New York	Amsterdam	Paris
Boston	Philadelphia	Jerusalem	Rome
Chicago	San Francisco	London	Stockholm
Los Angeles		Milan	Tokyo
		Moscow	Vienna

Referencing a Book With One Author

A reference for a book with one author appears as shown in Figure 82, and consists of the following elements:

- Author's last name

- Author's first initial, and middle initial, if available

- Year book was copyrighted

- Title of book

- City where publisher is located

- Name of publisher

To create this reference, follow these steps:

1. At the left margin, type the author's last name in full, followed by a comma and a space.

2. Type the author's first initial (*not* the full first name), followed by a period and a space, then the middle initial (if available), followed by a period and a space. If the author's middle name is not listed, just use the first initial.

Remember: *Never, never* use the full first name!

3. In parentheses, type the copyright year, followed by a period and a space.

4. Type the book title and italicize it. Only the first word has an initial capital letter; the rest of the words have initial lower-case letters unless they are proper names.

   If there is no subsequent edition, place a period after the title, then a space.

   If there is a subsequent edition, type a space, then an opening parenthesis, followed by the edition number in abbreviated format (i.e., 2nd, 3rd, 4th, etc.). Type the abbreviation "ed.," followed by a closing parenthesis and another period.

5. Type the city of publication, followed by a colon and a space. Include the two-letter state code or country name if the city is not listed in Table 15 on page 141 (i.e., Blue Ridge Summit, PA). For the state code abbreviation, see Table 14, page 54.

6. Type the publisher's name, followed by a period.

7. If your reference continues to a second line, double-space the second line and begin it at the left margin.

Follow this format exactly. See Appendix F for a complete list of references.

```
Parris, C. A. (1969). Mastering executive arts and

    skills. New York: Atheneum.
```

```
Parris, C. A. (1969). Mastering executive arts and

    skills (2nd ed.). New York: Atheneum.
```

Figure 82. Examples of a Reference of a Book with One Author.

Referencing a Book With Two Authors

A reference for a book with two authors appears as shown in Figure 83 and consists of the following elements:

- Both authors' last names

- Both authors' first initials and middle initials, if available

- Year book was copyrighted

- Title of book

- City where publisher is located

- Name of publisher

To create this reference, follow these steps:

1. At the left margin, type the first author's last name in full, followed by a comma and a space.

2. Type the first author's first initial (*not* the full first name), followed by a period and a space, then the middle initial (if available), followed by a period, a comma, and a space. If the author's middle name is not listed, just use the first initial.

Remember: *Never, never* use the full first name!

3. Type an ampersand (&) and a space.

4. Type the second author's last name, followed by a comma and a space.

5. Type the second author's first initial (*not* the full first name!), followed by a period and a space, then the middle initial (if available), followed by a period and a space. If the author's middle name is not listed, just use the first initial.

6. In parentheses, type the copyright year, followed by a period and a space.

7. Type the book title and italicize it. Only the first word has an initial capital letter; the rest of the words have initial lower-case letters unless they are proper names.

    Place a period after the title, then a space.

8. Type the city of publication, followed by a colon and a space. Include the two-letter state code or country name if the city is not listed in Table 15 on page 141 (i.e., Blue Ridge Summit, PA). For the state code abbreviation, see Table 14, page 54.

9. Type the publisher's name, followed by a period.

10. If your reference continues to a second line, double-space the second line and indent it three spaces.

Follow this format exactly. See Appendix F for a complete list of references.

```
Spetch, M. L., & Wilkie, D. M. (1983). How to

   bullet-proof your manuscript. New York: Atheneum.
```

Figure 83. Example of a Reference of a Book With Two Authors.

Referencing a Book With Three or More Authors

A reference for a book with three or more authors appears in the first example shown in Figure 84 and consists of the following elements:

- First six authors' first initials and middle initials, if available

- Year book was copyrighted

- Title of book

- City where publisher is located

- Name of publisher

To create this reference, follow these steps:

1. Type the first author's last name in full, followed by a comma and a space.

2. Type the first author's first initial (*not* the full first name), followed by a period and a space, then the middle initial (if available), followed by a period, a comma, and a space. If the author's middle name is not listed, just use the first initial.

Remember: *Never, never* use the full first name!

3. If there are three to six authors, continue with this step. If there are more than six, go to Step 4.

   Repeat Steps 1 and 2 for each author up to the second to the last. Type an ampersand (&), a space, then the last author's last name in full, followed by a comma and a space. Type the last author's first initial (*not* the full first name), followed by a period and a space, then the middle initial (if available), followed by a period, and a space. If the author's middle name is not listed, just use the first initial. Refer to the first example in Figure 84. Go to Step 5.

4. Repeat Steps 1 and 2 for the first six authors. Credit any remaining authors by using "et al," Type a period and a space. Refer to the second example in Figure 84.

5. In parentheses, type the copyright year, followed by a period.

6. Type the book title and italicize it. Only the first word has an initial capital letter; the rest of the words have initial lower-case letters unless they are proper names.

    Place a period after the title, then a space.

7. Type the city of publication, followed by a colon and a space. Include the two-letter state code or country name if the city is not listed in Table 15 on page 141 (i.e., Blue Ridge Summit, PA). For the state code abbreviation, see Table 14, page 54.

8. Type the publisher's name, followed by a period.

9. If your reference continues to a second line, double-space the second line and indent it three spaces.

    Follow this format exactly. See Appendix F for a complete list of references.

Sanders, T. J., Johnson, D. W., Adams, T., Russell,

   S., Berovic, M., & Motts, D. (1992). *Effective*

   leadership in the 90s. New York: Management Press.

Sanders, T. J., Johnson, D. W., Adams, T., Russell,

   S., Berovic, M., Motts, D., et al. (1994).

   Management problems in high-tech companies.

   New York: Management Press.

Figure 84. Examples of a Reference of a Book With Three or More Authors.

Referencing a Book With a Group Author (Company or Agency)

Some books are published with a company or government agency listed as the author. The American Management Association may publish a book, for instance, and list no author or editor other than itself.

A reference for a book with a group author is different from a reference of a book with an author. It appears as shown in Figure 85 and consists of the following elements:

- Name of publisher

- Year book was copyrighted

- Title of book

- City where publisher is located

- Word "Author"

To create this reference, follow these steps:

1. At the left margin, type the publisher's name (used in lieu of an author's name), followed by a period and a space.

2. In parentheses, type the copyright year, followed by a period and a space.

3. Type the book title, then italicize it. Only the first word has an initial capital letter; the rest of the words have initial lower-case letters unless they are proper names. Follow the title with a period and a space.

4. Type the city of publication, followed by a colon and a space. Include the two-letter state code or country name if the city is not listed in Table 15 on page 141 (i.e., Blue Ridge Summit, PA). For the state code abbreviation, see Table 14, page 54.

5. Type the word "Author," and begin it with a capital "A." This represents the publisher.

6. If your reference continues to a second line, double-space the second line and indent it three spaces.

Follow this format exactly. See Appendix F for a complete list of references.

```
American Management Association. (1992). PCs today.

    New York: Author.
```

Figure 85. Example of Reference of a Book With a Group Author.

Referencing a Book With an Editor

Many times, books are edited rather than authored; that is, they are a collection of articles or stories by other people, and the final book is put together by another person altogether. The cover and title page of the book will tell you that the person is the editor rather than the writer.

A reference for a book with an editor appears as shown in Figure 86 and consists of the following elements:

- Editor's last name

- Editor's first initial, and middle initial, if available

- Abbreviation "Ed."

- Year book was copyrighted

- Title of book

- City where publisher is located

- Name of publisher

To create this reference, follow these steps:

1. At the left margin, type the editor's last name in full, followed by a comma and a space.

2. Type the editor's first initial (*not* the full first name), followed by a period and a space, then the middle initial (if available), followed by a period, a comma, and a space. If the editor's middle name is not listed, just use the first initial.

Remember: *Never, never* use the full first name!

3. In parentheses, type the abbreviation "Ed.," followed by a space.

4. In parentheses, type the copyright year, followed by a period and a space.

5. Type the book title, then italicize it. Use an initial capital letter on the first word but use lower-case letters on the remaining words unless they are proper names. Follow the title with a period and a space.

6. Type the city of publication, a colon, and a space. Include the two-letter state code or country name if the city is not listed in Table 15 on page 141 (i.e., Blue Ridge Summit, PA). For the state code abbreviation, see Table 14, page 54.

7. Type the publisher's name, followed by a period.

8. If your reference continues to a second line, double-space the second line and indent it three spaces.

Follow this format exactly. See Appendix F for a complete list of references.

```
Jones, J. (Ed.). (1992). PCs today. New York:

   Doubleday.
```

Figure 86. Example of a Reference of a Book With an Editor.

Referencing a Book With an Author and an Editor

A reference for a book with an author and an editor appears as shown in Figure 87 and consists of the following elements:

- Author's last name

- Author's first initial, and middle initial, if available

- Year book was copyrighted

- Title of book

- Editor's first initial, and middle initial, if available

- Editor's last name

- City where publisher is located

- Name of publisher

To create this reference, follow these steps:

1. At the left margin, type the author's last name in full, followed by a comma and a space.

2. Type the author's first initial (*not* the full first name), followed by a period and a space, then the middle initial (if available), followed by a period and a space. If the author's middle name is not listed, just use the first initial.

Remember: *Never, never* use the full first name!

3. In parentheses, type the copyright year, followed by a period and a space.

4. Type the book title and italicize it. Only the first word has an initial capital letter; the rest of the words have initial lower-case letters unless they are proper names.

5. Type an opening parenthesis, the editor's first initial, a period and a space, and the middle initial (if available), followed by a period and a space. Type the editor's last name, followed by a comma and a space.

6. Type the abbreviation "Ed.," followed by a period, a closing parenthesis, and another period. Make sure the "E" is capitalized.

7.   Type the city of publication, followed by a colon and a space. Include the two-letter state code or country name if the city is not listed in Table 15 on page 141 (i.e., Blue Ridge Summit, PA). For the state code abbreviation, see Table 14, page 54.

8.   Type the publisher's name, followed by a period.

9.   If your reference continues to a second line, double-space the second line and indent it three spaces.

Follow this format exactly. See Appendix F for a complete list of references.

```
Harrison, P. R. (1989). The manager's world (F. G.

   Taylor, Ed.). Los Angeles: Business Press.
```

Figure 87. Example of a Reference of a Book with an Author and an Editor.

Referencing a Book With No Author or Editor

Many books do not list an author or editor at all, just the title. Most reference books fall in this category.

A reference for a book with no author is different from a reference of a book with an author. It appears as shown in Figure 88 and consists of the following elements:

- Title of book

- Edition, if relevant

- Abbreviation "ed."

- Year book was copyrighted

- City where publisher is located

- Publisher's name

To create this reference, follow these steps:

1. At the left margin, type the book title and italicize it. Only the first word has an initial capital letter; the rest of the words have initial lower-case letters unless they are proper names.

2. In parentheses, type the edition number and the abbreviation "ed." After the closing parenthesis, types a period and a space.

3. In parentheses, type the copyright year, followed by a period and a space.

4. Type the city of publication, followed by a colon and a space. Include the two-letter state or country name if the city is not listed in Table 15 on page 141 (i.e., Blue Ridge Summit, PA). For the state code abbreviation, see Table 14, page 54.

5. Type the publisher's name, followed by a period.

6. If your reference continues to a second line, double-space the second line and indent it three spaces.

Follow this format exactly. See Appendix F for a complete list of references.

The Wallace dictionary (4th ed.). (1992). New York:

    Wallace.

Figure 88. Example of a Reference of a Book With No Author or Editor.

Referencing a Book With a Subtitle

What if the book has a subtitle?

A reference for a book with a subtitle appears as shown in Figure 89 and consists of the following elements:

- Author's last name

- Author's first initial, and middle initial, if available

- Year book was copyrighted

- Title of book

- City where publisher is located

- Name of publisher

To create this reference, follow these steps:

1. At the left margin, type the author's last name in full, followed by a comma and a space.

    NOTE: *If this book has two authors, multiple authors, no author, an editor, etc., see the pages showing how to reference those forms.*

2. Type the author's first initial (*not* the full first name), followed by a period and a space, then the middle initial (if available), followed by a period and a space. If the author's middle name is not listed, just use the first initial.

Remember: *Never, never* use the full first name!

3. In parentheses, type the copyright year, followed by a period and a space.

4a. Type the title of the book, followed by a colon. Only the first word has an initial capital letter; the rest of the words have initial lower-case letters unless they are proper names.

   b. Type the subtitle, beginning once again with an initial capital letter. The remaining words have initial lower-case letters.

   c. Italicize the entire title.

   d. Place a period after the title, then a space.

5. Type the city of publication, followed by a colon and a space. Include the two-letter state or country name if the city is not listed in Table 15 on page 141 (i.e., Blue Ridge Summit, PA). For the state code abbreviation, see Table 14, page 54.

6. Type the publisher's name, followed by a period.

7. If your reference continues to a second line, double-space the second line and indent it three spaces.

Follow this format exactly. See Appendix F for a complete list of references.

```
Bernstein, T. M. (1965). The careful writer: A

    modern guide to English usage. New York: Atheneum.
```

Figure 89. Example of a Reference of a Book With a Subtitle.

Referencing an Article or Chapter in a Book

You can also reference an article or chapter within a book. A reference for an article or chapter within a book appears as shown in Figure 90 and consists of the following elements:

- Author's last name

- Author's first initial, and middle initial, if available

- Year book was copyrighted

- Title of article or chapter

- Name of book

- Page numbers of article or chapter

- City where publisher is located

- Name of publisher

To create this reference, follow these steps:

1. At the left margin, type the author's last name in full, followed by a comma and a space.

2. Type the author's first initial (*not* the full first name), followed by a period and a space, then the middle initial (if available), followed by a period, a comma, and a space. If the author's middle name is not listed, just use the first initial.

Remember: *Never, never* use the full first name!

3. In parentheses, type the copyright year, followed by a period and a space.

4. Type the title of the article. Use an initial capital letter on the first word but use initial lower-case letters on all the remaining words unless they are proper names. End the title with a period and a space.

5. Type the word "In" in plain type, followed by the book title. Only the first word of the title has an initial capital letter; the rest of the words have initial lower-case letters, unless they are proper names. Italicize the title. Follow it with a period and a space.

6. Type the page numbers in parentheses. Be sure to use "pp," followed by a period, if there is a range of pages. End with a period and a space.

7. Type the city of publication, followed by a colon and a space. Include the two-letter state code or country name if the city is not listed in Table 15 on page 141 (i.e., Blue Ridge Summit, PA). For the state code abbreviation, see Table 14, page 54.

8. Type the publisher's name, followed by a period.

9. If your reference continues to a second line, double-space the second line and indent it three spaces.

Follow this format exactly. See Appendix F for a complete list of references.

```
Jones, J. T. (1992). The workplace in the year 2000.

   In PCs today (pp. 113-120). New York: Doubleday.
```

Figure 90. Example of a Reference of an Article or Chapter in a Book.

Referencing an Article or Chapter in an Edited Book

You can also reference an article or chapter within an edited book. A reference for an article or chapter within an edited book appears as shown in Figure 91 and consists of the following elements:

- Author's last name

- Author's first initial, and middle initial, if available

- Year book was copyrighted

- Title of article or chapter

- Word "In"

- Editor's first initial, and middle initial, if available

- Editor's last name

- Name of book

- Page numbers of article or chapter

- City where publisher is located

- Name of publisher

To create this reference, follow these steps:

1. At the left margin, type the author's last name in full, followed by a comma and a space.

2. Type the author's first initial (*not* the full first name), followed by a period and a space, then the middle initial (if available), followed by a period and a space. If the author's middle name is not listed, just use the first initial.

   Remember: *Never, never* use the full first name!

3. In parentheses, type the copyright year, followed by a period and a space.

4. Type the title of the article. Use an initial capital letter on the first word but use lower-case letters on all the remaining words unless. End the title with a period and a space.

5. Type the word "In" in plain type, followed by the editor's first initial, a period, a space, and the editor's middle initial, if available, a period, and a space.

6. In parentheses, type the abbreviation, "Ed.," followed by a closing parenthesis, a comma, and a space as shown in the first example in Figure 91.

    If there are two editors, refer to the second example in Figure 91.

7. Type the book title and italicize it. Only the first word of the title has a capital letter; the rest are lower case, unless they are proper names.

8. Type the page numbers in parentheses. Be sure to use "pp," followed by a period, if there is a range of pages. End with another period.

9. Type the city of publication, followed by a colon and a space. Include the two-letter state code or country name if the city is not listed in Table 15 on page 141 (i.e., Blue Ridge Summit, PA). For the state code abbreviation, see Table 14, page 54.

10. Type the publisher's name, followed by a period.

11. If your reference continues to a second line, double-space the second line and indent it three spaces.

Follow this format exactly. See Appendix F for a complete list of references.

Jones, J. T. (1992). The workplace in the year 2000.

　　In S. L. Graves (Ed.), *PCs today* (pp. 201-210).

　　New York: Acme Press.

Jones, J. T. (1992). The workplace in the year 2000.

　　In S. L. Graves & D. G. Motts (Eds.), *PCs today*

　　(pp. 201-210). New York: Acme Press.

Figure 91. Examples of a Reference of an Article or Chapter in an Edited Book.

Referencing a Company Brochure

Most company brochures have no authors. A reference for a brochure appears as shown in Figure 92 and consists of the following elements:

- Name of company whose name appears on the brochure

- Year of publication, if available

- Title of brochure

- Number of edition, if applicable

- The word "Brochure"

- City and state where brochure was published

- The word "Author"

To create this reference, follow these steps:

1. At the left margin, type the company name, followed by a period and a space. Capitalize the first letter of all main words in the name.

2. In parentheses, type the copyright year, if available, followed by a period and a space.

3. In italics, type the title of the brochure. Use an initial capital letter on the first word but use lower-case letters on all the remaining words unless they are proper names. Follow it with a space.

4. If there is an edition number, type it in parentheses and follow it with a space.

5. In brackets, type the word "Brochure," followed by a period and a space. Capitalize the "B."

6. Type the city of publication, followed by a colon and a space. Include the two-letter state code or country name if the city is not listed in Table 15 on page 141 (i.e., Blue Ridge Summit, PA). For the state code abbreviation, see Table 14, page 54.

7. Type the word "Author," followed by a period. Capitalize the "A."

8. If your reference continues to a second line, double-space the second line and indent it three spaces.

Follow this format exactly. See Appendix F for a complete list of references.

```
Stanley Equipment Co. (1994). Ergonomic furniture

    for health and safety (2nd ed.) [Brochure]. New

    York: Author.
```

Figure 92. Example of a Reference of a Company Brochure.

Referencing Encyclopedias and Dictionaries

You can reference encyclopedias or dictionaries in four ways:

- With an author

- Without an author

- With an editor

- As an article in an encyclopedia

Referencing an Encyclopedia Set or Dictionary With an Author

A reference for an encyclopedia set or dictionary with an author appears as shown in Figure 93 and consists of the following elements:

- Author's last name

- Author's first and middle initials, if available

- Year encyclopedia set or dictionary was copyrighted

- Title of encyclopedia set or dictionary

- Number of edition, if relevant

- Volumes numbers, if encyclopedia set

- City where publisher is located

- Name of publisher

To create this reference, follow these steps:

1. At the left margin, type the author's last name in full, followed by a comma and a space.

2. Type the author's first initial (*not* the full first name), followed by a period and a space, then the middle initial (if available), followed by a period and a space.

Remember: *Never, never* use the full first name!

3. In parentheses, type the copyright year, followed by a period and a space.

4. In italics, type the encyclopedia set or dictionary title. Only the first word has an initial capital letter; the rest of the words have initial lower-case letters unless they are proper names. Follow the title with a space.

   If there is an edition number, go to Step 5. If there is no edition number, go to Step 5b.

5. Type an opening parenthesis, then the edition number, followed by a comma and a space. Abbreviate the word "edition" as "ed." (use lower-case letters). If there are volume numbers to reference, go to Step 5a. If there are not, go to Step 5b.

   a. Type the word "Volume(s)" as the abbreviated form "Vol.(s.)" and follow it with a space. Type the volume numbers.

   b. Type a closing parenthesis, followed by a period and a space.

6. Type the city of publication, followed by a colon and a space. Include the two-letter state code or country name if the city is not listed in Table 15 on page 141 (i.e., Blue Ridge Summit, PA). For the state code abbreviations, see Table 14, page 54.

7. Type the publisher's name, followed by a period.

8. If your reference continues to a second line, double-space the second line and indent it three spaces.

   Follow this format exactly. See Appendix F for a complete list of references.

```
Smith, R. F. (1994). Encyclopedia of ecology (3rd ed.,

    Vols. 1-10). New York: Acme.
```

```
Jones, T. M. (1992). Dictionary of computer terms

    (2nd ed.). New York: Times Books.
```

Figure 93. Examples of References of an Encyclopedia Set and Dictionary With an Author.

Referencing an Encyclopedia Set or Dictionary With No Author

A reference for an encyclopedia set or dictionary with no author appears as shown in Figure 94 and consists of the following elements:

- Publisher's name

- Year encyclopedia set or dictionary was copyrighted

- Title of encyclopedia set or dictionary

- Number of edition, if relevant

- Volumes numbers, if encyclopedia set

- City where publisher is located

To create this reference, follow these steps:

1. At the left margin, type the publisher's name in full, followed by a period and a space.

2. In parentheses, type the copyright year, followed by a period and a space.

3. In italics, type the encyclopedia set or dictionary title. Only the first word has an initial capital letter; the rest of the words have initial lower-case letters unless they are proper names. Follow the title with a period and a space.

   If there is an edition number, go to Step 4. If there is no edition number, go to Step 4b.

4. Type an opening parenthesis, then the edition number, followed by a comma and a space. Abbreviate the word "edition" as "ed." (use lower-case letters). If there are volume numbers to reference, go to Step 4a. If there are not, go to Step 4b.

   a. Type the word "Volume(s)" as the abbreviated form "Vol.(s.)" and follow it with a space. Type the volume numbers.

   b. Type a closing parenthesis, followed by a period and a space.

5. Type the city of publication, followed by a colon and a space. Include the two-letter state code or country name if the city is not listed in Table 15 on page 141 (i.e., Blue Ridge Summit, PA). For the state code abbreviation, see Table 14, page 54.

6. Type the word "Author" (to indicate that the publisher is the company listed in the place where the author normally goes), followed by a period.

7. If your reference continues to a second line, double-space the second line and indent it three spaces.

Follow this format exactly. See Appendix F for a complete list of references.

```
Acme. (1994). Encyclopedia of ecology (3rd ed.,

   Vols. 1-10). New York: Author.
```

```
Times Books. (1992). Dictionary of business terms

   (2nd ed.). New York: Author.
```

Figure 94. Examples of References of an Encyclopedia Set and Dictionary With No Author.

Referencing an Encyclopedia Set or Dictionary With an Editor

A reference for an encyclopedia set or dictionary with an editor appears as shown in Figure 95 and consists of the following elements:

- Editor's last name

- Editor's first and middle initials, if available

- Abbreviation "Ed."

- Year encyclopedia set or dictionary was copyrighted

- Title of encyclopedia set or dictionary

- Number of edition, if relevant

- Volume numbers, if encyclopedia set

- City where publisher is located

- Name of publisher

To create this reference, follow these steps:

1. At the left margin, type the editor's last name in full, followed by a comma and a space.

2. Type the editor's first initial (*not* the full first name), followed by a period and a space, then the middle initial (if available), followed by a period and a space. If the editor's middle name is not listed, just use the first initial.

Remember: *Never, never* use the full first name!

3. In parentheses, type the abbreviation "Ed.," followed by a period and a space.

4. In parentheses, type the copyright year, followed by a period and a space.

5. In italics, type the encyclopedia set or dictionary title. Only the first word has an initial capital letter; the rest of the words have initial lower-case letters unless they are proper names. Follow the title with a space.

6. Type an opening parenthesis, then the edition number, followed by a comma and a space. Abbreviate the word "edition" as "ed." (use lower-case letters). If there are volume numbers to reference, go to Step 6a. If there are not, go to Step 6b.

   a. Type the word "Volume(s)" as the abbreviated form "Vol.(s.)" and follow it with a space. Type the volume numbers.

   b. Type a closing parenthesis, followed by a period and a space.

7. Type the city of publication, followed by a colon and a space. Include the two-letter state code or country name if the city is not listed in Table 15 on page 141 (i.e., Blue Ridge Summit, PA). For the state code abbreviation, see Table 14, page 54.

8. Type the publisher's name, followed by a period.

9. If your reference continues to a second line, double-space the second line and indent it three spaces.

Follow this format exactly. See Appendix F for a complete list of references.

```
Smith, R. F. (Ed.). (1994). Encyclopedia of

    Ecology (3rd ed., Vols. 1-10). New York: Acme.
```

```
Jones, T. M. (Ed.). (1992). Dictionary of business

    terms (2nd ed.). New York: Times Books.
```

Figure 95. Examples of References of an Encyclopedia Set and Dictionary With an Editor.

Referencing an Article in an Encyclopedia

Articles in encyclopedias may or may not have an author. The following sections show you how to reference both types.

Referencing an Article With an Author in an Encyclopedia

A reference for an article with an author in an encyclopedia or encyclopedia set appears as shown in Figure 96 and consists of the following elements:

- Author's last name

- Author's first initial, and middle initial, if available

- Year encyclopedia or set was copyrighted

- Title of article

- Title of encyclopedia or set

- Number of edition, if relevant

- Volume number, if encyclopedia set

- City where publisher is located

- Name of publisher

To create this reference, follow these steps:

1. At the left margin, type the author's last name in full, followed by a comma and a space.

2. Type the author's first initial (*not* the full first name), followed by a period and a space, then the middle initial (if available), followed by a period and a space. If the author's middle name is not listed, just use the first initial.

Remember: *Never, never* use the full first name!

3. In parentheses, type the copyright year, followed by a period and a space.

4. Type the title of the article in plain type. Use an initial capital letter on the first word but use lower-case letters on the remaining words unless they are proper names. End the title with a period and a space.

5. Type the word "In" in plain type, using a capital "I." In italics, type the title of the encyclopedia or set. Only the first word has an initial capital letter; the rest of the words have initial lower-case letters unless they are proper names. Follow the title with a period and a space.

6. If there is a volume number to reference, continue with this step. If not, go to Step 7.

   Place the volume number in parentheses. Abbreviate the word "Volume" as "Vol.," followed by a space. Type the volume number, followed by a comma and a space. Type the letter "p," followed by a period and a space (or "pp.," if there is a range of pages). Type the page number(s), followed by a closing parenthesis, a period, and a space. Go to Step 8.

7. Type an opening parenthesis, then the letter "P," followed by a period (or "Pp.," if there is a range of pages). Type the page number(s), followed by a closing parenthesis, a period, and a space.

8. Type the city of publication, followed by a colon and a space. Include the two-letter state code or country name if the city is not listed in Table 15 on page 141 (i.e., Blue Ridge Summit, PA). For the state code abbreviation, see Table 14, page 54.

9. Type the publisher's name, followed by a period.

10. If your reference continues to a second line, double-space the second line and indent it three spaces.

Follow this format exactly. See Appendix F for a complete list of references.

Jamison, L. R. (1991). The disappearing ozone

layer. In *Encyclopedia of ecology.* (Vol. 4, pp.

22-27). New York: Acme.

Figure 96. Example of a Reference of an Article With an Author in an Encyclopedia.

Referencing an Article With No Author in an Encyclopedia

A reference for an article with no author in an encyclopedia appears as shown in Figure 97 and consists of the following elements:

- Title of article

- Year encyclopedia was copyrighted

- Title of encyclopedia

- Number of edition, if relevant

- Volume number, if encyclopedia set

- City where publisher is located

- Name of publisher

To create this reference, follow these steps:

1. At the left margin, type the title of the article in plain type. Use an initial capital letter on the first word but use lower-case letters on the remaining words unless they are proper names. End the title with a period and a space.

2. In parentheses, type the copyright year, followed by a period and a space.

3. Type the word "In" in plain type, using a capital "I." In italics, type the title of the encyclopedia or set. Only the first word has an initial capital letter; the rest of the words have initial lower-case letters unless they are proper names. Follow the title with a period and a space.

4. If there is a volume number to reference, continue with this step. If not, go to Step 5.

   Place the volume number in parentheses. Abbreviate the word "Volume" as "Vol.," followed by a space. Type the volume number, followed by a comma and a space. Type the letter "p," followed by a period and a space (or "pp.," if there is a range of pages). Type the page number(s), followed by a closing parenthesis, a period, and a space. Go to Step 6.

5. Type an opening parenthesis, then the letter "P," followed by a period (or "Pp.," if there is a range of pages). Type the page number(s), followed by a closing parenthesis, a period, and a space.

6. Type the city of publication, followed by a colon and a space. Include the two-letter state code or country name if the city is not listed in Table 15 on page 141 (i.e., Blue Ridge Summit, PA). For the state code abbreviation, see Table 14, page 54.

7. Type the publisher's name, followed by a period.

8. If your reference continues to a second line, double-space the second line and indent it three spaces.

Follow this format exactly. See Appendix F for a complete list of references.

```
The disappearing ozone layer. (1994). In Encyclopedia

   of ecology. (Vol. 4, pp. 22-27). New York: Acme.
```

Figure 97. Example of a Reference of an Article With No Author in an Encyclopedia.

Referencing Government Publications

This section shows you how to reference a report from the:

- Government Printing Office (GPO)

- National Technical Information Service (NTIS)

- Educational Resources Information Center (ERIC)

and a

- Government report not available from the GPO or a document deposit service

Referencing a Report From the Government Printing Office (GPO)

The Government Printing Office (GPO) prints all the publications from federal agencies. Many are available free or at a low-cost, and you may find these helpful in your research. A reference of a GPO publication appears in Figure 98 and consists of the following elements:

- Issuing agency's name

- Year report was copyrighted

- Title of report

- Number of report, if relevant

- Washington, DC

- U.S. Government Printing Office

To create this reference, follow these steps:

1. At the left margin, type the issuing agency's name in full, followed by a period and a space.

2. In parentheses, type the copyright year, followed by a period and a space. (Include the month, if relevant.)

3. In italics, type the report title. Only the first word has an initial capital letter; the rest of the words have initial lower-case letters unless they are proper names.

4. In parentheses, type the publication number. Abbreviate the word "number" as "No." After the closing parenthesis, type a period and a space.

5. Type "Washington, DC," followed by a colon, a space, and "U.S. Government Printing Office," followed by a period.

6. If your reference continues to a second line, double-space the second line and indent it three spaces.

Follow this format exactly. See Appendix F for a complete list of references.

Small Business Administration. (1976). *Checklist for*

going into business (Small Marketers Aid No. 71).

Washington, DC: U.S. Government Printing Office.

Figure 98. Example of a Reference of a Report From the Government Printing Office (GPO).

Referencing a Report From the National Technical Information Service (NTIS)

A reference of a National Technical Information Service (NTIS) publication appears in Figure 99 and consists of the following elements:

- Author's name(s)

- Year report was copyrighted

- Title of report

- Number of report, if relevant

- City of publication

- Publisher's name

To create this reference, follow these steps:

1. At the left margin, type the author's last name in full, followed by a comma and a space.

2. Type the author's first initial (*not* the full first name), followed by a period and a space, then the middle initial (if available), followed by a period and a space. If the author's middle name is not listed, just use the first initial.

   Remember: *Never, never* use the full first name!

3. In parentheses, type the copyright year, followed by a period and a space.

4. In italics, type the report title. Only the first word has an initial capital letter; the rest of the words have initial lower-case letters unless they are proper names. Follow the title with a period and a space.

5. Type the city where the university is located, followed by a comma and a space. Include the two-letter state code if the state is not part of the university name (i.e., Blue Ridge Summit, PA). For the state code abbreviation, see Table 14, page 54. See the first example in Figure 99. (Or include the country name if this is a foreign location).

You do not need to include the state code or country name if the name is part of the university's name. See the second example in Figure 99.

6. Type the publisher's name, followed by a period and a space.

7. In parentheses, type the publication number. Abbreviate the word "number" as "No."; however, do *not* place any punctuation after the closing parenthesis.

8. If your reference continues to a second line, double-space the second line and indent it three spaces.

Follow this format exactly. See Appendix F for a complete list of references.

```
Jones, J. T. (1993). Infant health problems in

    West Africa. Elm City, NV: University of the West.

(NTIS No. AA 10-444 300/AS)
```

```
Jones, J. T. (1993). Infant health problems in

    West Africa. Las Vegas: University of Nevada.

(NTIS No. AA 10-444 300/AS)
```

Figure 99. Examples of a Reference of a Report From the National Technical Information Service (NTIS).

Referencing a Report Available From the Educational Resources Information Center (ERIC)

A reference of a report available from the Educational Resources Information Center (ERIC) appears in Figure 100 and consists of the following elements:

- Author's name(s)

- Year report was copyrighted

- Title of report

- Number of report, if relevant

- City of publication

- Publisher's name

- ERIC document number

To create this reference, follow these steps:

1. At the left margin, type the author's last name in full, followed by a comma and a space.

2. Type the author's first initial (*not* the full first name), followed by a period and a space, then the middle initial (if available), followed by a period and a space. If the author's middle name is not listed, just use the first initial.

Remember: *Never, never* use the full first name!

3. In parentheses, type the copyright year, followed by a period and a space.

4. Type the report title in italics. Only the first word has an initial capital letter; the rest of the words have initial lower-case letters unless they are proper names.

   If there is a report number, type a space and go to Step 5. If there isn't, type a period and a space and go to Step 6.

5. In parentheses, type the report number and follow the closing parenthesis with a period and a space.

6. Type the city of publication, followed by a colon and a space. Include the two-letter state code or country name if the city is not listed in Table 15 on page 141 (i.e., Blue Ridge Summit, PA). For the state code abbreviation, see Table 14, page 54.

7. Type the publisher's name, followed by a period and a space.

8. In parentheses, type the ERIC number. Abbreviate the word "number" as "No." Do *not* place any punctuation after the closing parenthesis.

9. If your reference continues to a second line, double-space the second line and indent it three spaces.

Follow this format exactly. See Appendix F for a complete list of references.

```
Berovic, V. (2001). Reading scores in one-room schools

   in the southern states (Report No. 4528). Elm City,

   NV: University of the West. (ERIC Document

   Reproduction Service No. ED123456)
```

Figure 100. Example of a Reference of a Report From the Educational Resources Information Center (ERIC).

Referencing a Government Report Not Available From the GPO or a Document Deposit Service

A reference of a government report not available from the GPO or a Document Deposit Service appears in Figure 101 and consists of the following elements:

- Name of the issuing agency

- Year report was copyrighted

- Title of report

- Number of report, if relevant

- City of publication

- Publisher's name or word "Author"

To create this reference, follow these steps:

1. At the left margin, type the name of the issuing agency, followed by a period and a space.

2. In parentheses, type the copyright year, followed by a period and a space.

3. Type the report title in italics. Only the first word has an initial capital letter; the rest of the words have initial lower-case letters unless they are proper names. If the report has a number, follow the title with a space and go to Step 4. If it does not have a number, follow it with a period and a space and go to Step 5.

4. If the report has a number, type it in parentheses, and follow it with a period and a space.

5. Type the city of publication, followed by a colon and a space. Include the two-letter state code or country name if the city is not listed in Table 15 on page 141 (i.e., Blue Ridge Summit, PA). For the state code abbreviation, see Table 14, page 54.

6. Type the publisher's name, followed by a period. If the author is the issuing agency, type the word "Author" here, as shown in Figure 101.

7. If your reference continues to a second line, double-space the second line and indent it three spaces.

Follow this format exactly. See Appendix F for a complete list of references.

```
Small Business Administration (2001). Statistics on

    Attendees at Seminars Presented in Orange County

    (SBA Publication No. 12765-43). Santa Ana, CA:

    Author.
```

Figure 101. Example of a Government Report Not Available From the GPO or a Document Deposit Service.

Referencing a Report From a Private Organization

Private organizations are institutes, foundations, etc. A reference of a report from a private organization appears in Figure 102 and consists of the following elements:

- Organization's name

- Year report was copyrighted (and month, if applicable)

- Title of report

- Number of report, if relevant

- City where the organization is located

- The word "Author"

To create this reference, follow these steps:

1. At the left margin, type the organization's name in full, followed by a period and a space.

2. In parentheses, type the copyright year. Include the month, if available, as shown in Figure 101. Type a period and a space.

3a. In italics, type the report title. Only the first word has an initial capital letter; the rest of the words have initial lower-case letters unless they are proper names.

  b. In parentheses, type "Issue No." and the issue number, if available, followed by the closing parenthesis, a period, and a space.

4. Type the city of publication, followed by a colon and a space. Include the two-letter state code or country name if the city is not listed in Table 15 on page 141 (i.e., Blue Ridge Summit, PA). For the state code abbreviation, see Table 14, page 54.

5. Type the word "Author" and a period.

6. If your reference continues to a second line, double-space the second line and indent it three spaces.

Follow this format exactly. See Appendix F for a complete list of references.

Manufacturing Institute. (1993, December). *Changes*

in management philosophy from 1980 to 1990 (Issue

No. 6). Main City, IA: Author.

Figure 102. Example of a Reference of a Report From a Private
Organization.

Referencing Academic Material

This section shows you how to reference:

- a report from a university

- proceedings of meetings and symposia

- an unpublished paper presented at a meeting

- doctoral dissertations and master's theses

Referencing a Report From a University

A reference of a report from a university appears in Figure 103 and consists of the following elements:

- Author's name(s)

- Year report was copyrighted

- Title of report

- Number of report, if relevant

- City where the university is located

- University's name

- Name of the department issuing the report

To create this reference, follow these steps:

1. At the left margin, type the author's last name in full, followed by a comma and a space.

2. Type the author's first initial (*not* the full first name), followed by a period, a space, then the middle initial (if available), then another period and a space. If the author's middle name is not listed, just use the first initial.

Remember: *Never, never* use the full first name!

3. In parentheses, type the copyright year, followed by a period and a space.

4a. Type the report title and italicize it. Only the first word has an initial capital letter; the rest of the words have initial lower-case letters unless they are proper names. Follow the title with a space.

b. Place the publication number in parentheses. Abbreviate any words associated with it; abbreviate the word "number" as "No.," followed by a space.

c. After the closing parenthesis, type a period and a space.

5. Type the city of publication, followed by a comma, a space, then the two-letter state code from Table 14 on page 54 (or country name, if this is a foreign publication), a colon, and a space. (If the state is included in the university's name, you do not need to repeat the state name here.)

6. Type the name of the university, followed by a comma and a space.

7. Type the name of the department issuing the report, followed by a period.

8. If your reference continues to a second line, double-space the second line and indent it three spaces.

Follow this format exactly. See Appendix F for a complete list of references.

```
Jones, J. T. (1993). Changes in management philosophy

   from 1980 to 1990 (Tech. Rep. No. 6). Main City, IA:

   Eastern State University, School of Business.
```

Figure 103. Example of a Reference of a Report From a University.

Referencing Proceedings of Meetings and Symposia

Your sources may include proceedings from a meeting or symposium. These can be in the following forms:

- Published proceedings

- Published contribution to a symposium

- Article or chapter in an edited book

- Proceedings published regularly

- Unpublished contribution to a symposium

- Unpublished paper presented at a meeting

Referencing Published Proceedings, Published Contribution to a Symposium, or Article or Chapter in an Edited Book

A reference for published proceedings, a published contribution to a symposium, or an article or chapter in an edited book appears as shown in Figure 104, and consists of the following elements:

- Author's last name

- Author's first initial, and middle initial, if available

- Year proceedings were published

- Title of article

- Word "In"

- Name of editor, if relevant, and abbreviation "Ed."

- Name of proceedings, symposium, or book

- City of publication

- Publisher's name

To create this reference, follow these steps:

1. At the left margin, type the author's last name in full, followed by a comma and a space.

2. Type the author's first initial (*not* the full first name), followed by a period and a space, then the middle initial (if available), followed by a period and a space. If the author's middle name is not listed, just use the first initial.

   Remember: *Never, never* use the full first name!

3. In parentheses, type the copyright year, followed by a period and a space.

4. In italics, type the title of the article. Use an initial capital letter on the first word but use lower-case letters on all the remaining words unless they are proper names. End the title with a period and a space.

5. Type the word "In" in plain type, followed by a space. If there is an editor, continue with this step. If not, go to Step 6. In parentheses, type the editor's name in first initial, middle initial, last name format, a space, and the abbreviation "Ed.," followed by a comma and a space.

6. In italics, type the title of the proceedings or book. Only the first word of the title has an initial capital letter; the rest of the words have initial lower-case letters, unless they are proper names.

7. In parentheses, type the page numbers. Be sure to use "pp," followed by a period, if there is a range of pages. Follow this with another period and a space.

8. Type the city of publication, followed by a colon and a space. Include the two-letter state code or country name if the city is not listed in Table 15 on page 141 (i.e., Blue Ridge Summit, PA). (If the state is included in the university's name, you do not need to repeat the state name here.)

9. Type the publisher's name, followed by a period.

10. If your reference continues to a second line, double-space the second line and indent it three spaces.

Follow this format exactly. See Appendix F for a complete list of references.

Johnson, D. J. (1999). *Mastering executive arts and*

   skills. In D. Adams (Ed.), *Orange County*

   Symposium on Business Management (pp. 45-52).

   Irvine: University of California Press.

Figure 104. Example of a Reference of Published Proceedings, a Published Contribution to a Symposium, or an Article or Chapter in an Edited Book.

Referencing Proceedings Published Regularly

To reference proceedings that are published at regular intervals, use the same formats as those for periodicals.

Referencing an Unpublished Contribution to a Symposium

A reference for an unpublished contribution to a symposium appears as shown in Figure 105 and consists of the following elements:

- Author's last name

- Author's first initial, and middle initial, if available

- Year paper was presented

- Title of paper

- Word "In"

- Name of symposium chair

- Word "Chair"

- Title of symposium

- Words "Symposium conducted at"

- Name of symposium

To create this reference, follow these steps:

1. At the left margin, type the author's last name in full, followed by a comma and a space.

2. Type the author's first initial (*not* the full first name), followed by a period and a space, then the middle initial (if available), followed by a period and a space. If the author's middle name is not listed, just use the first initial.

   Remember: *Never, never* use the full first name!

3. Type an opening parenthesis, the year the paper was presented, a comma, then the month and a closing parenthesis, followed by a period and a space.

4. Type the title of the article. Use an initial capital letter on the first word but use lower-case letters on all the remaining words unless they are proper names. Follow the title with a period and a space.

5. Type the word "In," followed by a space and the name of the symposium chair, in first initial, middle initial (if available), last name format, followed by a space.

6. In parentheses, type the word "Chair," followed by a comma and a space. Use an initial capital "C" on this word.

7. In italics, type the name of the symposium. Only the first word of the title has a capital letter; the rest of the words have initial lower-case letters, unless they are proper names.

8. Type the words "Symposium conducted at," followed by the name of the meeting or conference at which the symposium was conducted. End with a comma and a space.

9. Type the city where the symposium was held, followed by a comma, a space, then the two-letter state code from Table 14 on page 54 (or country name, if this is a foreign location), a colon, and a space.

10. If your reference continues to a second line, double-space the second line and indent it three spaces.

Follow this format exactly. See Appendix F for a complete list of references.

Johnson, D. J. (2002, June). Mastering executive arts

    and skills. In D. Adams (Chair), *Orange County*

    Symposium on Business Management. Symposium

    conducted at the Third Annual Conference on

    Business Management, Irvine, CA.

Figure 105. Example of a Reference of an Unpublished Contribution to a Symposium.

Referencing an Unpublished Paper Presented at a Meeting

A reference for an unpublished paper presented at a meeting appears as shown in Figure 106, and consists of the following elements:

- Author's last name

- Author's first initial, and middle initial, if available

- Year paper was presented

- Title of paper

- Words "Paper presented at the meeting of the"

- Name of meeting

- City and state (or country) were meeting was held

To create this reference, follow these steps:

1. At the left margin, type the author's last name in full, followed by a comma and a space.

2. Type the author's first initial (*not* the full first name), followed by a period and a space, then the middle initial (if available), followed by a period and a space. If the author's middle name is not listed, just use the first initial.

    Remember: *Never, never* use the full first name!

3. Type an parenthesis, then the year the paper was presented, followed by a comma and a space, then the month, followed by the closing parenthesis, a period, and a space.

4. Type the title of the article. Use an initial capital letter on the first word but use lower-case letters on all the remaining words unless they are proper names. Follow the title with a comma and a space.

5. Type the words "Paper presented at the meeting of the," followed by a space.

6. Type the name of the organization sponsoring the meeting, followed by a comma and a space.

7. Type the city where the meeting was held, followed by a comma, a space, then the two-letter state code from Table 14 on page 54 (or country name, if this is a foreign location), a colon, and a space.

8. If your reference continues to a second line, double-space the second line and indent it three spaces.

Follow this format exactly. See Appendix F for a complete list of references.

```
Amato, C. J. (1975, April). Perspectives on a

   Future Human Society. Paper presented at the

   meeting of the American Astronautical Society,

   San Francisco, CA.
```

Figure 106. Example of a Reference of an Unpublished Paper Presented at a Meeting.

Referencing a Doctoral Dissertation

This section shows you how to reference a(n):

- Published doctoral dissertation abstracted in Dissertation Abstracts International (DAI) and

  - ❑ obtained from University Microfilm

  - ❑ obtained from the university

- Unpublished doctoral dissertation

Referencing a Published Dissertation Abstracted in Dissertation Abstracts International (DAI) and Obtained From UMI

Check Dissertation Abstracts International (DAI) to see what other students have done on your topic. University Microfilm, Inc. (UMI) keeps microfilm copies of all dissertations created in the United States. A reference of a published dissertation abstracted in DAI and obtained from UMI appears in Figure 107 and consists of the following elements:

- Author's name(s)

- Year dissertation was copyrighted

- Title of dissertation

- Words "Dissertation Abstracts International"

- Volume number

- Page and series number

- UMI number

To create this reference, follow these steps:

1. At the left margin, type the author's last name in full, followed by a comma and a space.

2. Type the author's first initial (*not* the full first name), a period, a space, the middle initial (if available), then another period and a space. If the author's middle name is not listed, just use the first initial.

Remember: *Never, never* use the full first name!

3. In parentheses, type the copyright year, followed by a period and a space.

4. Type the dissertation title, followed by a period and a space. Only the first word has an initial capital letter; the rest of the words have initial lower-case letters unless they are proper names.

5. Type the words "Dissertation Abstracts International," a comma, and a space. Type the volume number. Italicize all of these elements.

6. If the issue number is available, type it in parentheses, followed by a comma and a space. If there is no issue number, just type the comma and the space.

7. Type the page number and the series number (A is for humanities; B is for sciences), followed by a period and a space. (If there is no issue number, be sure to include "p." before the page number (or "pp." for a range of pages)).

8. In parentheses, type the UMI reference number in parentheses. Abbreviate the word "Number" as "No." Do not end the phrase with any punctuation.

9. If your reference continues to a second line, double-space the second line and indent it three spaces.

Follow this format exactly. See Appendix F for a complete list of references.

Jones, J. T. (1993). The effects of bottom-up management

   techniques on clerical employees in five high-tech

   companies. *Dissertation Abstracts International,*

   53(01), 236B. (University Microfilms No. AAD93-12345)

Figure 107. Example of a Reference of a Published Dissertation Abstracted in DAI and Obtained From UMI.

Referencing a Dissertation Abstracted in Dissertation Abstracts International (DAI) and Obtained From the University

A reference of a published dissertation abstracted in Dissertation Abstracts International (DAI) and obtained from the university appears in Figure 108 and consists of the following elements:

- Author's name(s)

- Year dissertation was copyrighted in DAI

- Title of dissertation

- Words "Doctoral Dissertation"

- Name of the university

- Year on the cover page of the dissertation

- Words "Dissertation Abstracts International"

- Volume number

- Page number(s)

To create this reference, follow these steps:

1. At the left margin, type the author's last name in full, followed by a comma and a space.

2. Type the author's first initial (*not* the full first name), a period, a space, the middle initial (if available), then another period and a space. If the author's middle name is not listed, just use the first initial.

   Remember: *Never, never* use the full first name!

3. Type the DAI copyright year in parentheses, followed by a period and a space.

4. Type the dissertation title. Only the first word has an initial capital letter; the rest of the words have initial lower-case letters unless they are proper names. Follow the title with a period and a space.

5. Type an opening parenthesis, then the words "Doctoral dissertation," followed by a comma and a space.

6. Type the name of the university, followed by a comma and a space.

7. Type the year on the cover page of the dissertation, followed by a closing parenthesis, a period, and a space.

8. Type the words "Dissertation Abstracts International," a comma, a space, the volume number, and a comma. Italicize all of these elements.

9. Type a space, then the DAI page numbers.

10. If your reference continues to a second line, double-space the second line and indent it three spaces.

Follow this format exactly. See Appendix F for a complete list of references.

Jones, J. T. (1993). The effects of bottom-up

management techniques on clerical employees in five

high-tech companies. (Doctoral dissertation, Eastern

State University, 1993). *Dissertation Abstracts*

International, 53, 3023.

Figure 108. Example of a Reference of a Dissertation Abstracted in DAI and Obtained From the University.

Referencing an Unpublished Dissertation

You might get some material from a dissertation on which someone is currently working. A reference of a unpublished dissertation appears in Figure 109 and consists of the following elements:

- Author's name(s)

- Year in which the material was written

- Title of dissertation

- Words "Unpublished doctoral dissertation"

- Name of the university

- City (and two-letter state code, if not in the university name) where the university is located

To create this reference, follow these steps:

1. At the left margin, type the author's last name in full, followed by a comma and a space.

2. Type the author's first initial (*not* the full first name), a period, a space, the middle initial (if available), then another period and a space. If the author's middle name is not listed, just use the first initial.

   Remember: *Never, never* use the full first name!

3. Type the year in which the material was written in parentheses, followed by a period and a space.

4. Type the dissertation title and italicize it. Only the first word has an initial capital letter; the rest of the words have initial lower-case letters unless they are proper names. End with a period and a space.

5. Type the words "Unpublished doctoral dissertation," followed by a comma and a space.

6. Type the name of the university, followed by a comma and a space.

7. Type the city in which the university is located. Include the two-letter state code (see Table 14, p. 54) if the state is not in the university name. Follow this with a period.

8.   If your reference continues to a second line, double-space the second line and indent it three spaces.

Follow this format exactly. See Appendix F for a complete list of references.

Jones, J. T. (1993). *The effects of bottom-up management*

techniques on clerical employees in five high-tech

companies. Unpublished doctoral dissertation,

Eastern State University, Elm City, CT.

Figure 109. Example of a Reference of an Unpublished Dissertation.

Referencing a Master's Thesis

This section shows you how to reference a(n):

- Published master's thesis abstracted in Master's Abstracts International (MAI) and obtained from University Microfilm (UMI)

- Published master's thesis abstracted in Master's Abstracts International (MAI) and obtained from the university

- Unpublished master's thesis

Referencing a Published Thesis Abstracted in Master's Abstracts International (MAI) and Obtained From UMI

Check Master's Abstracts International (MAI) to see what other students have done on your topic. UMI keeps microfilm copies of all theses created in the United States. A reference of a published thesis abstracted in MAI and obtained from UMI appears in Figure 110 and consists of the following elements:

- Author's name(s)

- Year thesis was copyrighted

- Title of thesis

- Words "Master's Abstracts International"

- Volume number

- Page number

- UMI number

To create this reference, follow these steps:

1. At the left margin, type the author's last name in full, followed by a comma and a space.

2. Type the author's first initial (*not* the full first name), a period, a space, the middle initial (if available), then another period and a space. If the author's middle name is not listed, just use the first initial.

Remember: *Never, never* use the full first name!

3. In parentheses, type the copyright year, followed by a period and a space.

4. Type the thesis title, followed by a period and a space. Only the first word has an initial capital letter; the rest of the words have initial lower-case letters unless they are proper names.

5. Type the words "Master's Abstracts International," a comma, a space, the volume number, and a comma. Italicize all of these elements.

6. Type a space and the page number, followed by a period.

7. In parentheses, type the University Microfilms reference number in parentheses. Abbreviate the word "Number" as "No." Do not include any punctuation after the closing parenthesis.

8. If your reference continues to a second line, double-space the second line and indent it three spaces.

Follow this format exactly. See Appendix F for a complete list of references.

```
Jones, J. T. (1993). The effects of bottom-up

   management techniques on clerical employees in five

   companies. Master's Abstracts International,

   53, 236. (UMI No. AAD93-12345)
```

Figure 110. Example of a Reference of a Published Master's Thesis Abstracted in MAI and Obtained From UMI.

Referencing a Thesis Abstracted in Master's Abstracts International (MAI) and Obtained From the University

A reference of a published thesis abstracted in MAI and obtained from the university appears in Figure 111 and consists of the following elements:

- Author's name(s)

- Year thesis was copyrighted in DAI

- Title of thesis

- Words "Master's Thesis"

- Name of the university

- Year on the cover page of the dissertation

- Words "Master's Abstracts International"

- Volume number

- Page number(s)

To create this reference, follow these steps:

1. At the left margin, type the author's last name in full, followed by a comma and a space.

2. Type the author's first initial (*not* the full first name), a period, a space, the middle initial (if available), then another period and a space. If the author's middle name is not listed, just use the first initial.

Remember: *Never, never* use the full first name!

3. Type the MAI copyright year in parentheses, followed by a period and a space.

4. Type the thesis title, followed by a period and a space. Only the first word has an initial capital letter; the rest of the words have initial lower-case letters unless they are proper names.

5. Type an opening parenthesis, then the words "Master's thesis," followed by a comma and a space.

6. Type the name of the university, followed by a comma and a space.

7. Type the year on the cover page of the thesis, followed by a closing parenthesis, a space, and a period.

8. Type the words "Master's Abstracts International," a comma, a space, and the volume number. Italicize all of these elements.

9. Type a comma and a space.

10. Type the MAI page number and a period.

11. If your reference continues to a second line, double-space the second line and indent it three spaces.

Follow this format exactly. See Appendix F for a complete list of references.

```
Jones, J. T. (1993). The effects of bottom-up

   management techniques on clerical employees in five

   high-tech companies. (Master's thesis, Eastern State

   University, 1993). Master's Abstracts International,

   53, 642B.
```

Figure 111. Example of a Reference of a Master's Thesis Abstracted in MAI and Obtained From the University.

Referencing an Unpublished Master's Thesis

You might get some material from a thesis on which someone is currently working. A reference of a unpublished thesis appears in Figure 112 and consists of the following elements:

- Author's name(s)

- Year in which the thesis was written

- Title of thesis

- Words "Unpublished master's thesis"

- Name of the university

- City (and two-letter state code, if not in the university name) where the university is located

To create this reference, follow these steps:

1. At the left margin, type the author's last name in full, followed by a comma and a space.

2. Type the author's first initial (*not* the full first name), a period, a space, the middle initial (if available), then another period and a space. If the author's middle name is not listed, just use the first initial.

   Remember: *Never, never* use the full first name!

3. In parentheses, type the year in which the material was written, followed by a period and a space.

4. In italics, type the thesis title, followed by a period. Only the first word of the title has an initial capital letter; the rest of the words have initial lower-case letters unless they are proper names.

5. Type the words "Unpublished master's thesis" in parentheses, followed by a comma and a space.

6. Type the name of the university, followed by a comma and a space.

7. Type the city in which the university is located. Follow it with a comma and a space and the two-letter state code if the state is not in the university name. (See Table 14, page 54, for the two-letter state code abbreviations.)

8. If your reference continues to a second line, double-space the second line and indent it three spaces.

Follow this format exactly. See Appendix F for a complete list of references.

Jones, J. T. (1993). *The effects of bottom-up management techniques on clerical employees in five high-tech companies.* Unpublished master's thesis, Eastern State University, Elm City, CT.

Figure 112. Example of a Reference of an Unpublished Master's Thesis.

Referencing an Unpublished Manuscript Not Submitted for Publication

You might get some material from a manuscript on which someone is currently working. A reference of a unpublished manuscript not submitted for publication appears in Figure 113 and consists of the following elements:

- Author's name(s)

- Year in which the manuscript was written

- Title of manuscript

- Words "Unpublished manuscript"

To create this reference, follow these steps:

1. At the left margin, type the author's last name in full, followed by a comma and a space.

2. Type the author's first initial (*not* the full first name), a period, a space, the middle initial (if available), then another period and a space. If the author's middle name is not listed, just use the first initial.

   Remember: *Never, never* use the full first name!

3. In parentheses, type the year in which the material was written, followed by a period and a space.

4. In italics, type the manuscript title. Only the first word of the title has an initial capital letter; the rest of the words have initial lower-case letters unless they are proper names. Follow the title with a period and a space.

5. Type the words "Unpublished manuscript," followed by a period.

6. If your reference continues to a second line, double-space the second line and indent it three spaces.

Follow this format exactly. See Appendix F for a complete list of references.

Jones, J. T. (1993). *The effects of bottom-up management techniques on clerical employees in five high-tech companies.* Unpublished manuscript.

Figure 113. Example of a Reference of an Unpublished Manuscript Not Submitted for Publication.

Referencing a Manuscript in Progress or Submitted for Publication But Not Yet Accepted

You might get some material from a manuscript that is in progress or has been submitted for publication but has not yet been accepted. A reference of a manuscript in progress or submitted for publication, but not yet accepted is shown in Figure 114 and consists of the following elements:

- Author's name(s)

- Year in which the thesis was written

- Title of thesis

- Words "Manuscript in progress" or "Manuscript submitted for publication"

To create this reference, follow these steps:

1. At the left margin, type the author's last name in full, followed by a comma.

2. Type the author's first initial (*not* the full first name), a period, a space, the middle initial (if available), then another period and a space. If the author's middle name is not listed, just use the first initial.

Remember: *Never, never* use the full first name!

3. In parentheses, type the year in which the material was written, followed by a period and a space.

4. In italics, type the thesis title, followed by a period. Only the first word of the title has an initial capital letter; the rest of the words have initial lower-case letters unless they are proper names.

5. Type the words "Manuscript in progress" or "Manuscript submitted for publication," whichever is applicable. End with a period.

6. If your reference continues to a second line, double-space the second line and indent it three spaces.

Follow this format exactly. See Appendix F for a complete list of references.

Jones, J. T. (1993). *The effects of bottom-up management techniques on clerical employees in five high-tech companies.* Manuscript submitted for publication.

Figure 114. Example of a Reference of a Manuscript Submitted for Publication But Not Yet Accepted.

Referencing Unpublished Raw Data From a Study

You might get some material from data someone has collected but has not published. A reference of raw data from a study that does not have an official published title appears in Figure 115 and consists of the following elements:

- Author's name(s)

- Year in which the material was written

- Title of study

- Words "Unpublished raw data"

To create this reference, follow these steps:

1. At the left margin, type the author's last name in full, followed by a comma and a space.

2. Type the author's first initial (*not* the full first name), a period, a space, the middle initial (if available), then another period and a space. If the author's middle name is not listed, just use the first initial.

Remember: *Never, never* use the full first name!

3. In parentheses, type the year in which the material was written, followed by a period and a space.

4. In brackets, type the topic to indicate that this is a description of the content, not a title. Only the first word has an initial capital letter; the rest of the words have initial lower-case letters unless they are proper names.

5. Type a space, then the words "Unpublished raw data," followed by a period.

6. If your reference continues to a second line, double-space the second line and indent it three spaces.

Follow this format exactly. See Appendix F for a complete list of references.

Finlayson, F. D. (1993). [The effects of bottom-up

management techniques on clerical employees in five

high-tech companies.] Unpublished raw data.

Figure 115. Example of a Reference of Unpublished Raw Data From a Study.

Referencing Reviews

This section shows you how to reference a:

- book review

- movie review

- video review

Referencing a Book Review

A reference of a book review appears as shown in Figure 116 and consists of the following elements:

- Author's name(s)

- Year in which the review was copyrighted

- Title of review, if available

- Words "Review of the book"

- Book title

- Name of the magazine or newspaper in which the review appeared

- Volume number, if relevant

- Page number(s)

To create this reference, follow these steps:

1. At the left margin, type the author's last name in full, followed by a comma and a space.

2. Type the author's first initial (*not* the full first name), a period, a space, the middle initial (if available), then another period and a space. If the author's middle name is not listed, just use the first initial.

Remember: *Never, never* use the full first name!

3. In parentheses, type the year in which the review was written, followed by a period and a space.

4. If the review has a title, continue with this step. If not, go to Step 5.

    Type the title. Only the first word has an initial capital letter; the rest of the words have initial lower-case letters unless they are proper names.

5. Type an opening bracket, the words "Review of the book," and the book title, followed by a closing bracket, a period, and a space. Use lower-case letters on all words in the title except the first unless it contains a proper name. Italicize all the words in the book title.

6. Type the name of the magazine or newspaper in which the review appeared and follow it with a comma, a space, the volume number, and a comma. Italicize all of these.

7. Type a space, then the page numbers, followed by a period. (If there is no volume number, be sure to include the "P." (or "Pp." for a range of pages) before the page numbers.)

8. If your reference continues to a second line, double-space the second line and indent it three spaces.

    Follow this format exactly. See Appendix F for a complete list of references.

Jones, J. T. (1993). Exploring new management tech-

   niques. [Review of the book *The bottom-up approach*].

   Today's Business, 24, 25-26.

Figure 116. Example of a Reference of a Book Review.

Referencing a Movie Review

A reference of a movie review appears as shown in Figure 117 and consists of the following elements:

- Author's name(s)

- Year in which the review was copyrighted

- Title of review, if available

- Words "Review of the film"

- Movie title

- Name of the magazine or newspaper in which the review appeared

- Volume number, if relevant

- Page number(s)

To create this reference, follow these steps:

1. At the left margin, type the author's last name in full, followed by a comma and a space.

2. Type the author's first initial (*not* the full first name), a period, a space, the middle initial (if available), then another period and a space. If the author's middle name is not listed, just use the first initial.

Remember: *Never, never* use the full first name!

3. In parentheses, type the year in which the review was written, followed by a period and a space.

4. If the review has a title, continue with this step. If not, go to Step 5.

   Type the title. Only the first word has an initial capital letter; the rest of the words have initial lower-case letters unless they are proper names.

5. In brackets, type the words "Review of the film" and the film title, followed by a period and a space. Italicize the film title.

6. Type the name of the magazine or newspaper in which the review appeared, a comma, a space, and the volume number, if relevant, followed by a comma and a space. Italicize all of these.

7. Type the page number(s), followed by a period. (If there is no volume number, be sure to include the "P." (or "Pp." for a range of pages) before the page numbers.)

8. If your reference continues to a second line, double-space the second line and indent it three spaces.

Follow this format exactly. See Appendix F for a complete list of references.

Johnson, D. W. (1993). Sexual harassment in today's

corporate world. [Review of the movie *Disclosure*].

Today's Business, 26, 63-64.

Figure 117. Example of a Reference of a Movie Review.

Referencing a Video Review

A reference of a video review appears as shown in Figure 118 and consists of the following elements:

- Author's name(s)

- Year in which the review was copyrighted

- Title of review, if available

- Words "Review of the video"

- Video title

- Name of the magazine or newspaper in which the review appeared

- Volume number, if relevant

- Page number(s)

To create this reference, follow these steps:

1. At the left margin, type the author's last name in full, followed by a comma and a period.

2. Type the author's first initial (*not* the full first name), a period, a space, the middle initial (if available), then another period and a space. If the author's middle name is not listed, just use the first initial.

Remember: *Never, never* use the full first name!

3. In parentheses, type the year in which the review was written, followed by a period and a space.

4. If the review has a title, continue with this step. If not, go to Step 5.

    Type the title. Only the first word has an initial capital letter; the rest of the words have initial lower-case letters unless they are proper names. Follow the title with a period.

5. In brackets, type the words "Review of the video" and the video title, followed by a period and a space. Italicize the video title.

6. Type the name of the magazine or newspaper in which the review appeared, a comma, a space, and the volume number, if relevant. Italicize all of these elements.

7. Type a comma and a space, then the page numbers, followed by a period. (If there is no volume number, be sure to include the "P." (or "Pp." for a range of pages) before the page numbers.)

8. If your reference continues to a second line, double-space the second line and indent it three spaces.

Follow this format exactly. See Appendix F for a complete list of references.

Jones, J. T. (1993). Exploring new management

techniques. [Review of the video *The bottom-up*

approach]. *Today's Business, 24,* 25-26).

Figure 118. Example of a Reference of a Video Review.

Referencing Audio-Visual Materials

This section shows you how to reference a:

- movie

- television broadcast

- television series

- single episode from a television series

- cassette recording

You may find a lot of useful information for your report or project from these sources.

Referencing a Movie

A reference of a movie appears as shown in Figure 119 and consists of the following elements, which you can obtain from the movie's credits:

- Originator's name(s) and title(s)

- Year in which the movie was copyrighted

- Movie title

- Words "Motion picture"

- Words "Available from"

- Distributor's name and address, if relevant

To create this reference, follow these steps:

1. At the left margin, type the originator's last name in full, followed by a comma and a space. The originator can be the executive producer, producer, and/or the director.

2. Type the originator's first initial (*not* the full first name), a period, a space, the middle initial (if available), then a period and a space. If the originator's middle name is not listed, just use the first initial.

Remember: *Never, never* use the full first name!

3. In parentheses, type the originator's title, followed by a period and a space. (If there are two originators, see the second example in Figure 119.)

4. In parentheses, type the year in which the movie was copyrighted, followed by a period and a space.

5. Type the movie title, italicize it, and follow it with a space. Only the first word has a capital letter; the rest of the words have initial lower-case letters, unless they are proper names.

6. In brackets, type the words "Motion picture," followed by a period. Be sure to use a capital "M."

7. In parentheses, type the words "Available from," followed by the name of the distributor, a comma, a space, the distributor's street address, a comma, a space, and the city where the distributor is located.

8. If your reference continues to a second line, double-space the second line and indent it three spaces.

Follow this format exactly. See Appendix F for a complete list of references.

Smith, R. L. (Producer). (1993). *The great chase.*

   [Motion picture]. Available from Four Star

   Productions, 1567 Hollywood Boulevard, Hollywood,

   CA.

Smith, R. L. (Producer), & Jones, L. (Director).

   (1993). *Managing employees in 90s* [Motion picture].

   Available from Green Tree Business Productions, 1234

   Main Street, Elm City, CT.

Figure 119. Examples of a Reference of a Movie.

Referencing a Television Broadcast

A reference of a television broadcast appears as shown in Figure 120 and consists of the following elements, which you can obtain from the broadcast's credits:

- Originator's name and title

- Year and date of broadcast

- Television broadcast title

- Words "Television Broadcast"

- Name of the city from which the broadcast originated

- Production company name

To create this reference, follow these steps:

1. At the left margin, type the originator's last name in full, followed by a comma and a space. The originator can be the executive producer, producer, and/or the director.

2. Type the originator's first initial (*not* the full first name), a period, a space, the middle initial (if available), then a period and a space. If the originator's middle name is not listed, just use the first initial.

    Remember: *Never, never* use the full first name!

3. Type the originator's title in parentheses, followed by a period and a space.

4. In parentheses, type the year in which the show was broadcast, a comma, a space, the month the show was broadcast, the day (do not add "th" or "st"), a closing parenthesis, a period, and a space.

5. Type the television show title, a period, and a space. Italicize both. Only the first word has a capital letter; the rest of the words have initial lower-case letters, unless they are proper names.

6. In brackets, type the words "Television broadcast," followed by a period and a space.

7. Type the city or cities (for example: New York and Los Angeles) from which the broadcast originated, followed by a colon and a space.

8. Type the name of the production company, followed by a period.

9. If your reference continues to a second line, double-space the second line and indent it three spaces.

Follow this format exactly. See Appendix F for a complete list of references.

```
Smith, R. L. (Producer). (1993, August 4). The

   business report. [Television broadcast]. New York:

   National Broadcasting Company.
```

Figure 120. Example of a Reference of a Television Broadcast.

Referencing a Television Series

A reference of a television series appears as shown in Figure 121 and consists of the following elements, which you can obtain from the broadcast's credits:

- Originator's name and title

- Year the series aired

- Television series title

- Words "Television series"

- Name of the city from which the series was produced

- Production company name

To create this reference, follow these steps:

1. At the left margin, type the originator's last name in full, followed by a comma and a space. The originator can be the executive producer, producer, and/or the director.

2. Type the originator's first initial (*not* the full first name), a period, a space, the middle initial (if available), then a period and a space. If the originator's middle name is not listed, just use the first initial.

Remember: *Never, never* use the full first name!

3. Type the originator's title in parentheses, followed by a period.

4. In parentheses, type the year in which the show was broadcast, followed by a period.

5. Type the television show title and a period. Italicize both. Only the first word has a capital letter; the rest of the words have initial lower-case letters, unless they are proper names.

6. In brackets, type the words "Television broadcast," followed by a period and a space.

7. Type the city or cities (for example: New York and Los Angeles) from which the broadcast originated, followed by a colon and a space.

8. Type the name of the production company, followed by a period.

9. If your reference continues to a second line, double-space the second line and indent it three spaces.

Follow this format exactly. See Appendix F for a complete list of references.

```
Smith, R. L. (Producer). (1993). The human experience.

   [Television series]. New York: Public Broadcasting

   Service.
```

Figure 121. Example of a Reference of a Television Series.

Referencing an Episode From a Television Series

A reference of an episode from a television series appears as shown in Figure 122 and consists of the following elements, which you can obtain from the broadcast's credits:

- Scriptwriter's name

- Director's name

- Year the episode aired

- Episode title

- Words "Television series episode"

- Originator's name

- Originator's title

- Series title

- Name of the city from which the series was produced

- Production company name

To create this reference, follow these steps:

1. At the left margin, type the scriptwriter's last name in full, followed by a comma and a space.

2. Type the scriptwriter's first initial (*not* the full first name), a period, a space, the middle initial (if available), then a period and a space. If the scriptwriter's middle name is not listed, just use the first initial. Type a space, then in parentheses, type the word "Writer," followed by another space.

Remember: *Never, never* use the full first name!

3. Type an ampersand and another space, then the director's last name in full, followed by a comma and a space.

4. Type the director's first initial (*not* the full first name), a period, a space, the middle initial (if available), then a period and a space. If the director's middle name is not listed, just use the first initial. Type a space, then in parentheses, type the word "Director," followed by a period and a space.

5. In parentheses, type the year in which the show was broadcast, followed by a period and a space.

6. Type the episode title in italics. Only the first word has a capital letter; the rest of the words have initial lower-case letters, unless they are proper names. Follow the title with a space.

7. In brackets, type the words "Television series episode," followed by a period and a space.

8. Type the word "In," followed by the originator's first initial and last name, followed by a space.

9. In parentheses, type the originator's title. (The originator may be the producer or executive producer.) Type a capital letter on the first word of the title. After the closing parenthesis, type a comma and a space.

10. In italics, type the television series title, followed by a period and a space. Only the first word has a capital letter; the rest of the words have initial lower-case letters, unless they are proper names.

11. Type the city or cities from which the broadcast originated, followed by a colon and a space.

12. Type the name of the production company, followed by a period.

13. If your reference continues to a second line, double-space the second line and indent it three spaces.

Follow this format exactly. See Appendix F for a complete list of references.

Johnson, D. W. (Writer) & Smith, R. L. (Director).

   (1993). *The mysterious mind* [Television series

   episode]. In T. Harrison (Executive producer),

   The human experience. Los Angeles: Public

   Broadcasting Service.

Figure 122. Example of a Reference of an Episode From a Television Series.

Referencing a Cassette Recording

You may listen to a talk on a cassette that you will find useful in your research. A reference of cassette recording appears as shown in Figure 123 and consists of the following elements, which you can obtain from the cassette label or box cover:

- Primary contributor's or originator's name

- Primary contributor's or originator's title

- Copyright year

- Cassette title

- Words "Cassette Recording No."

- Recording number

- Name of the city where the cassette was produced

- Production company name

To create this reference, follow these steps:

1. At the left margin, type the primary contributor's or originator's last name in full, followed by a comma and a space.

2. Type the primary contributor's or originator's first initial (*not* the full first name), a period, a space, the middle initial (if available), then a period and a space. If the speaker's middle name is not listed, just use the first initial.

Remember: *Never, never* use the full first name!

3. In parentheses, type the primary contributor's or originator's title, followed by a period and a space. (In Figure 123, the primary contributor was the speaker.)

4. In parentheses, type the copyright year of the cassette, followed by a period and a space.

5. Type the cassette title and italicize it. Only the first word has a capital letter; the rest of the words have initial lower-case letters, unless they are proper names. Type a space.

6. In parentheses, type the words "Cassette Recording No.," followed by a space. Capitalize the "C," "R," and "N," and abbreviate the word "number" as No."

7. Type the cassette recording number, followed by a period and a space.

8. Type the city or cities from which the broadcast originated, followed by a colon and a space.

9. Type the name of the production company, followed by a period.

10. If your reference continues to a second line, double-space the second line and indent it three spaces.

Follow this format exactly. See Appendix F for a complete list of references.

Smith, R. L. (Speaker). (1993). *Management Tips for*

  the 90s (Cassette Recording No. 100-233-66A-B). New

  York: Acme Recording Company.

Figure 123. Example of a Reference of a Cassette Recording.

Referencing Legal Material

There are several types of legal references:

- Court cases

- Statutes

- Legislative materials

- Administrative and executive materials

- Patents

The APA requires that legal citations be referenced with the same information provided in conventional legal formats in legal periodicals. Unlike legal periodicals, however, which list legal citations in footnotes at the bottom of the page, the APA style guide requires legal references to be listed in the References.

For more information on referencing legal materials, please consult the 17th edition of *The Bluebook: A Uniform System of Citation* (2000), which the APA follows for legal citation style.

Referencing Court Cases

There are four main types of court cases:

- Court decisions

- Unpublished cases

- Court cases at the trial level

- Court cases at the appellate level

Common abbreviations used in legal references are shown in Table 16. When using these abbreviations, follow the spacing shown exactly.

Table 16. Abbreviations Used in Court References.

ABBREVIATION	MEANING
v.	versus
Cong.	U. S. Congress
H.R.	House of Representatives
S.	Senate
Reg.	Regulation
Res.	Resolution
aff'd	affirmed
F.	*Federal Reporter*
F.2d	*Federal Reporter, Second Series*
F. Supp.	*Federal Supplement*
U.S.C.	*United States Code*
Cong. Rec.	*Congressional Record*
Fed. Reg.	*Federal Register*
WL	Westlaw
Jan.	January
Feb.	February
Aug.	August
Sept.	September
Oct.	October
Nov.	November
Dec.	December

Referencing a Court Decision (*Bluebook* Rule 10)

A reference for a court decision appears as shown in Figure 124, and consists of the following elements:

- Name of the decision

- Source volume number

- Source name

- Source page number

- Court name

- Court date

To create this reference, follow these steps:

1. At the left margin, type the name of the decision, followed by a comma and a space. Be sure to use "v." in the decision name.

2. Type the volume number of the published source in which this case is listed, followed by a space.

3a. Type the source name in abbreviated format, followed by a space.

 b. Type the source page number, followed by a space.

4. In parentheses, type the court name and a space. (In Figure 124, "D. Calif." stands for District of California). Type the date.

5. If your reference continues to a second line, double-space the second line and indent it three spaces.

Follow this format exactly. See Appendix F for a complete list of references.

```
Smith v. Jones, 234 F. Supp. 1394 (D. Calif. 1984).
```

Figure 124. Example of a Reference of a Court Decision.

Referencing an Unpublished Case

There are two types of unpublished cases:

- Filed but not yet reported

- Unreported decision

Referencing a Case That is Filed But Not Yet Reported

A reference for a case that is filed but not yet reported appears as shown in Figure 125 and consists of the following elements:

- Case name

- Docket number

- Court name in which case was filed

- Word "filed"

- Date of filing

1. At the left margin, type the name of the case, followed by a comma and a space.

2. Type the docket number, followed by a space. Use the Abbreviate "Number" as "No."

3a. In parentheses, type the name of the court in which the case was filed, followed by a space.

b. Type the word "filed," followed by a space.

c. Type the date of filing, followed by a space. (Refer to Table 16 on page 227 to see if the month should be abbreviated.) Type a period and a space. Type the day, followed by a comma and a space, then the year, followed by the closing parenthesis and a period.

4. If your reference continues to a second line, double-space the second line and indent it three spaces.

Follow this format exactly. See Appendix F for a complete list of references.

```
Smith v. Jones, No. 23-1004 (U.S. filed March 3, 1993).
```

Figure 125. Example of a Reference of a Case That is Filed But Not Reported.

Referencing an Unreported Decision

You can reference an unreported decision from two sources:

- In print

- On LEXIS or Westlaw

REFERENCING AN UNREPORTED DECISION IN PRINT

A reference for an unreported decision in print appears as shown in Figure 126, and consists of the following elements:

- Case name

- Docket number

- Words "slip op. at" (if relevant)

- Page number

- Name of the court

- Date of announcement

To create this reference, follow these steps:

1. At the left margin, type the name of the case, followed by a comma, and a space.

2. Type the docket number. Abbreviate "Number" as "No." End with a comma, and a space.

3. A "slip opinion" is an opinion not published in a case reporter, but printed separately, due to its recentness. If you wish to cite to a slip opinion, refer to the second example in Figure 126. Type the words "slip op. at," followed by a space.

4. In brackets, type the page number on which the case appears, followed by a space.

5. In parentheses, type the name of the court in which the case was filed, followed by a space.

6. Type the date of filing, followed by the closing parenthesis and a period. (See Table 16 on page 227 to see if the month should be abbreviated.)

7.   If your reference continues to a second line, double-space the
     second line and indent it three spaces.

Follow this format exactly. See Appendix F for a complete list of
references.

```
Smith v. Jones, No. 23-1004 (U.S. Dist. March 3, 1993).
```

```
Smith v. Jones, No. 23-1004, slip op. at [10]. (9th

   Cir. March 3, 1993).
```

Figure 126. Examples of a Reference of an Unreported Decision in Print.

REFERENCING AN UNREPORTED DECISION ON LEXIS OR WESTLAW

You can find unreported cases on LEXIS or Westlaw, too. These electronic databases are a tremendous resource for finding legal materials. A reference of an unreported decision found here may or may not have a record number.

Referencing an Unreported Decision on LEXIS or Westlaw With a Record Number

A reference with a record number appears as shown in Figure 127, and consists of the following elements:

- Case name

- Docket number

- Decision year

- Court name

- LEXIS or Westlaw record number

- Screen page number

- District name

- Date of decision

To create this reference, follow these steps:

1. At the left margin, type the name of the case, followed by a comma, and a space.

2. Type the docket number, a comma, and a space. Abbreviate "Number" as "No."

3. Type the decision year and court name.

4. Type the LEXIS or Westlaw record number, a comma, and a space.

5. Type the word "at," a space, an asterisk, and the screen page number. (The asterisk is used to distinguish this page number from a slip op page number.)

6a. In parentheses, type the name of the court in which the case was filed.

   b. Type the date of filing. (See Table 16 on page 227 to see if the month should be abbreviated.) Follow the date with a comma, a space, the year, the closing parenthesis, and a period.

   7. If your reference continues to a second line, double-space the second line and indent it three spaces.

   Follow this format exactly. See Appendix F for a complete list of references.

```
Gomez v. Sanders Corp., No. 45-1234, 1993 U.S. Dist.

   WL 19284, at *4 (D. Kan. Dec. 13, 1993).
```

Figure 127. Example of a Reference of an Unpublished Decision Found on Westlaw With a Record Number.

Referencing an Unreported Decision on LEXIS or Westlaw With No Record Number

A reference of an unreported decision on LEXIS or Westlaw without a record number appears as shown in Figure 128, and consists of the following elements:

- Case name

- Docket number

- Court name

- Date of decision

- Source name and other identifying information

To create this reference, follow these steps:

1. At the left margin, type the name of the case, followed by a comma, and a space.

2. Type the docket number and a space.

3a. In parentheses, type the name of the court in which the case was filed, followed by a period and a space.

  b. Type the date of filing. (Refer to Table 16 on page 227 to see if the month should be abbreviated.) Type a closing parenthesis and a space.

4. In parentheses, type the database name and any other identifying information.

5. If your reference continues to a second line, double-space the second line and indent it three spaces.

Follow this format exactly. See Appendix F for a complete list of references.

```
Williams v. ABC Manufacturing, No.12-4567 (D. Calif.

   June 25, 1994) (LEXIS, Genfed library, Dist file).
```

Figure 128. Example of a Reference of an Unpublished Case Found on LEXIS With No Record Number.

Referencing a Court Case at the Trial Level

You can reference trials at two levels:

- State trial court

- Federal district court

Referencing a State Trial Court Case

A reference of a state trial court case appears as shown in Figure 129, and consists of the following elements:

- Case name

- Source volume number

- Source name

- Source page number

- Court name

- Year of decision

To create this reference, follow these steps:

1. At the left margin, type the name of the case, followed by a comma and a space.

2a. Type the source volume number and a space.

b. Type the source name and a space. Note that the series number (4th) is right next to the source name abbreviation.

c. Type the source page number and a space.

3. In parentheses, type the court name and decision date, followed by a period.

4. If your reference continues to a second line, double-space the second line and indent it three spaces.

Follow this format exactly. See Appendix F for a complete list of references.

```
Williams v. ABC Manufacturing, 14 Ore. D. & C.4th 136

   (C.P. Multnomah County 1991).
```

Figure 129. Example of a Reference of a State Trial Court Case.

Referencing a Federal District Court Case

A reference of a federal district court case appears as shown in Figure 130, and consists of the following elements:

- Case name

- Source volume number

- Source name

- Source page number

- Court name

- Year of decision

To create this reference, follow these steps:

1. At the left margin, type the name of the case, followed by a comma and a space.

2a. Type the source volume number and a space.

b. Type the source name and a space.

c. Type the source page number and a space.

3. In parentheses, type the court name and decision date, followed by a period.

4. If your reference continues to a second line, double-space the second line and indent it three spaces.

Follow this format exactly. See Appendix F for a complete list of references.

```
Williams v. ABC Manufacturing, 456 F. Supp. 234

   (D. Calif. 1989).
```

Figure 130. Example of a Reference of a Federal District Court Case.

Referencing a Court Case at the Appellate Level

Court cases can be appealed to one of two courts:

- State supreme court
- State court of appeals

Referencing a Court Case Appealed to a State Supreme Court

A reference of a court case appealed to a state supreme court appears as shown in Figure 131, and consists of the following elements:

- Case name
- Source volume number
- Source name
- Source page number
- Year of decision

To create this reference, follow these steps:

1. At the left margin, type the name of the case, followed by a comma, and a space.

2a. Type the source volume number and a space.

  b. Type the source name and a space.

  c. Type the source page number and a space.

3. In parentheses, type the decision date, followed by a period.

4. If your reference continues to a second line, double-space the second line and indent it three spaces.

Follow this format exactly. See Appendix F for a complete list of references.

```
Williams v. ABC Manufacturing, 456 Calif. 234 (1989).
```

Figure 131. Example of a Reference of a Court Case Appealed to a State Supreme Court.

Referencing a Court Case Appealed to a State Court of Appeals

A reference of a court case appealed to a state court of appeals appears as shown in Figure 132, and consists of the following elements:

- Case name

- Source volume number

- Source name

- Source page number

- Court name

- Year of decision

To create this reference, follow these steps:

1.   At the left margin, type the name of the case, followed by a comma, and a space.

2a. Type the source volume number and a space.

  b. Type the source name and a space.

  c. Type the source page number and a space.

3.   In parentheses, type the court name and decision date, followed by a period.

4.   If your reference continues to a second line, double-space the second line and indent it three spaces.

Follow this format exactly. See Appendix F for a complete list of references.

```
Williams v. ABC Manufacturing, 902 S.W.2d 234

     (Calif. Ct. App. 1996).
```

Figure 132. Example of a Reference of a Court Case Appealed to a State Court of Appeals.

Referencing Statutes

You can reference statutes from two sources:

- State code

- Federal code

Referencing a Statute in a State Code

A reference for a statute in a state code appears as shown in Figure 133 and consists of the following elements:

- Name of act

- Volume number

- Source

- Section number

- Any other references to the act

To create this reference, follow these steps:

1. At the left margin, type the name of the act, followed by a comma and a space.

2. Type the volume number, followed by a space.

3. Type the source name, followed by a space.

4. Type the section symbol(s), followed by a space, and the section number(s), followed by a comma.

5. In parentheses, type any other references to the act, followed by a period.

6. If your reference continues to a second line, double-space the second line and indent it three spaces.

Follow this format exactly. See Appendix F for a complete list of references.

```
Health Care and Reform Act, 8 Calif. Stat. Ann.

   §§ 24-8763-8201 (1999 & Supp. 2001).
```

Figure 133. Example of a Reference of a Statute in a State Code.

Referencing a Statute in a Federal Code

A reference for a statute in a federal code appears as shown in Figure 134 and consists of the following elements:

- Name of act and year passed

- Volume number

- Source

- Section number

- Publisher of volume, if relevant

- Year volume was published

To create this reference, follow these steps:

1. At the left margin, type the name of the act, followed by a comma and a space.

2. Type the volume number, followed by a space.

3. Type the source name, followed by a space.

4. Type the section symbol, followed by a space, and the section number.

5. In parentheses, type the publisher's name, if relevant, a space, and the year the volume was published, followed by a period.

6. If your reference continues to a second line, double-space the second line and indent it three spaces.

Follow this format exactly. See Appendix F for a complete list of references.

```
National Environmental Policy Act of 1969, 44 U.S.C.A.

   § 4332 (West 1976).
```

Figure 134. Example of a Reference of a Statute in a Federal Code.

Referencing Legislative Materials (Bluebook Rule 13)

Legislative materials include:

- testimony at hearings

- full hearings

- unenacted federal bills and resolutions

- enacted bills and resolutions

- federal reports and documents

Referencing Testimony at a Hearing

A reference for testimony at a hearing appears as shown in Figure 135 and consists of the following elements:

- Title of hearing as stated on official pamphlet

- Congressional number

- Session number

- Page number of pamphlet

- Year testimony was given

- Words "testimony of" and the testifier's name

To create this reference, follow these steps:

1. At the left margin, type the hearing title, followed by a period and a space. Include the bill number, if relevant; the subcommittee name, if relevant; and the committee name. Italicize this entire entry.

2. Type the Congressional number, followed by a comma and a space.

3. Type the session number, followed by a space.

4. Type the page number in the pamphlet where the testimony is documented.

5. In parentheses, type the year in which the testimony was given.

6. In parentheses, type the name of the person whose testimony you are referencing. End with a period.

7. If your reference continues to a second line, double-space the second line and indent it three spaces.

Follow this format exactly. See Appendix F for a complete list of references.

RU486: The Import Ban and Its Effect on Medical Research: Hearings Before the Subcommittee on Regulation, Business Opportunities, and Energy, of the House Committee on Small Business. 101st Cong., 2d Sess. 35 (1990) (testimony of Ronald Chesemore).

Figure 135. Example of a Reference of Testimony at a Hearing.

Referencing a Full Hearing

A reference for a full hearing appears as shown in Figure 136 and consists of the following elements:

- Title of hearing as stated on official pamphlet

- Congressional number

- Session number

- Page number of pamphlet

- Year testimony was given

To create this reference, follow these steps:

1. At the left margin, type the hearing name, followed by a period and a space. Include the bill number, if relevant; the subcommittee name, if relevant; and the committee name. Italicize this entire entry.

2. Type the Congressional number, followed by a comma and a space.

3. Type the session number, followed by a space.

4. Type the page number in the pamphlet where the testimony is documented.

5. In parentheses, type the year in which the testimony was given. End with a period.

6. If your reference continues to a second line, double-space the second line and indent it three spaces.

Follow this format exactly. See Appendix F for a complete list of references.

RU486: The Import Ban and Its Effect on Medical Research: Hearings Before the Subcommittee on Regulation, Business Opportunities, and Energy, of the House Committee on Small Business. 101st Cong., 2d Sess. 35 (1990).

Figure 136. Example of a Reference of a Full Hearing.

Referencing an Unenacted Federal Bill or Resolution

A reference for an unenacted federal bill or resolution appears as shown in Figure 137 and consists of the following elements:

- Title, if available

- Source name

- Bill or resolution number

- Congressional or Senate number

- Session number

- Abbreviation "Sess."

- Section number, if relevant

- Year bill or resolution was introduced

To create this reference, follow these steps:

1. At the left margin, type the bill or resolution name, followed by a comma and a space.

2. Type the source name ("H.R." for House of Representatives or "S." for Senate), a space, and the bill or resolution number, followed by a comma and a space.

3. Type the Senate or Congressional number (use just "d" for "second" or "third"), followed by a comma and a space.

4. Type "Sen" for "Senate," or "Cong" for Congress, followed by a period and a space.

5. Type the session number (use just "d" for "second" or "third"), followed by a space and the abbreviation "Sess." for "session."

6. In parentheses, type the section symbol, a space, and the section number.

7. In parentheses, type the year in which the bill or resolution was introduced.

8. If your reference continues to a second line, double-space the second line and indent it three spaces.

Follow this format exactly. See Appendix F for a complete list of references.

```
Space Memorial Bill, H.R. 5936, 102d Cong., 2d

   Sess. (1992).
```

Figure 137. Example of a Reference of an Unenacted Federal Bill or Resolution.

Referencing an Enacted Federal Bill or Resolution

A reference for an enacted federal bill or resolution appears as shown in Figure 138 and consists of the following elements:

- Source and title, if available

- Bill or resolution number

- Congressional or Senate number

- Abbreviation "Cong." or "Sen."

- Session number

- Abbreviation "Sess." for "Session"

- Volume number

- Source

- Page number

- Year bill or resolution was passed

To create this reference, follow these steps:

1. At the left margin, type the source name ("H.R. Res." for House of Representatives Resolution or "S. Res." for Senate Resolution) and the bill or resolution number, followed by a comma and a space.

2. Type the Congressional or Senate number, followed by a comma and a space.

3. Type the abbreviation "Cong." or "Sen.," followed by a space.

4. Type the session number, followed by a space.

5. Type the abbreviation "Sess.," followed by a space.

6. Type the source volume number, followed by a space.

7. Type the source name in abbreviated form, followed by a space.

8. Type the page number, followed by a space.

9. In parentheses, type the year in which the bill or resolution was passed.

10. If your reference continues to a second line, double-space the second line and indent it three spaces.

Follow this format exactly. See Appendix F for a complete list of references.

```
S. Res. 5936, 102d Cong., 1st Sess. 139 Cong. Rec.

   4325 (1993) (enacted).
```

Figure 138. Example of a Reference of an Enacted Federal Bill or Resolution.

Referencing a Federal Report or Document

A reference for a federal report or document appears as shown in Figure 139 and consists of the following elements:

- Report or document number

- Congressional number

- Session number

- Year report or document was published

To create this reference, follow these steps:

1. At the left margin, type the source name ("H.R. Rep." or "H.R. Doc." for House of Representatives Report or Document, or "S. Rep." or "S. Doc." for Senate Report or Document) and the report or document number, followed by a comma and a space.

2. Type the Congressional number, followed by a comma and a space.

3. Type the session number, followed by a space.

4. Type the year in which the report or document was published.

5. If your reference continues to a second line, double-space the second line and indent it three spaces.

Follow this format exactly. See Appendix F for a complete list of references.

```
S. Rep. No. 104-234 at 10 (1993).
```

or

```
S. Doc. No. 104-234 at 10 (1993).
```

Figure 139. Examples of a Reference of a Federal Report or Document.

Referencing Administrative and Executive Materials

You can reference two types of administrative and executive materials:

- Federal rules and regulations

- Executive orders

Referencing a Federal Rule or Regulation

A reference for a federal rule or regulation appears as shown in Figure 140 and consists of the following elements:

- Title of the rule or regulation

- Number of the rule or regulation

- Volume number

- Source

- Section number

- Year in which the rule or regulation was passed

To create this reference, follow these steps:

1. At the left margin, type the rule or regulation title (and number, if relevant), a comma and a space.

2. Type the volume number, followed by a space, then the abbreviation "C. F. R." (Code of Federal Regulations).

3. Type the section symbol, a space, and the section number, followed by a space.

4. In parentheses, type the year the rule or regulation was passed.

5. If your reference continues to a second line, double-space the second line and indent it three spaces.

Follow this format exactly. See Appendix F for a complete list of references.

```
FTC Credit Practices Rule, 16 C.F.R. § 444 (1991).
```

Figure 140. Example of a Reference of a Federal Regulation.

Referencing an Executive Order

A reference for an executive order appears as shown in Figure 141 and consists of the following elements:

- Executive order number

- Volume number of the Code of Federal Regulations

- Page number

- Year in which the executive order was passed

To create this reference, follow these steps:

1. At the left margin, type the executive order number, a comma, and a space. Abbreviate as "Exec. Order No."

2. Type the volume number, followed by a space, then the abbreviation "C. F. R." (Code of Federal Regulations), followed by another space.

3. Type the page number, followed by a space.

4. In parentheses, type the year the executive order was issued, followed by a period.

5. If your reference continues to a second line, double-space the second line and indent it three spaces.

Follow this format exactly. See Appendix F for a complete list of references.

```
Exec. Order No. 12,804, 3 C.F.R. 298 (1992).
```

Figure 141. Example of a Reference of an Executive Order.

Referencing a Patent

A reference for a patent appears as shown in Figure 142 and consists of the following elements:

- Name of inventor

- Year patent was issued

- Words "U. S. Patent No." and the patent number

- City and office where patent was issued

To create this reference, follow these steps:

1. At the left margin, type the author's last name in full, followed by a comma and a space.

2. Type the author's first initial (*not* the full first name), a period, a space, the middle initial (if available), then a period and a space.

    Remember: *Never, never* use the full first name!

3. In parentheses, type the year the patent was issued, followed by a period and a space.

4. In italics, type the patent number, followed by a period and a space.

5. Type the city where the patent was issued. (In the U.S., this will be Washington, D.C.)

6. Type the office where the patent was issued. (In the U.S., this will be the U.S. Patent and Trademark Office.)

7. If your reference continues to a second line, double-space the second line and indent it three spaces.

Follow this format exactly. See Appendix F for a complete list of references.

Midgley, T. (1924). *U.S. Patent No. 1,501,568.*

Washington, DC: U.S. Patent and Trademark Office.

Figure 142. Example of a Reference of a Patent.

Referencing Electronic Media

You probably will find a lot of your source information from the Internet. This section shows you how to reference the following online sources:

- e-mail

- periodicals

- non-periodical documents

- messages on newsgroups, online forums and discussion groups, and electronic mailing lists

- proceedings of meetings and symposia

- technical/research reports

- computer programs, software, and programming languages

- raw data

- aggregated databases

Referencing e-mail

Since e-mails do not provide retrievable data to a reader, they are not included in the reference list. They are cited in the text only and follow the same format as a personal communication (see page 68).

Referencing Periodicals

The following items are classified as periodicals:

- An article in an Internet-only journal

- Internet articles based on a print source

- An article in an Internet-only journal, retrieved via FTP

- An article in an Internet-only Newsletter

Referencing an Article in a Journal Available Only on the Internet

A reference of an article from a journal available only on the Internet appears as shown in Figure 143 and consists of the following elements:

- Author's last name

- Author's first initial, and middle initial, if available

- Date of publication (year, month, day)

- Title of article

- Title of journal

- Volume number

- Article number

- Words "Retrieved from"

- Date document was retrieved

- URL

To create this reference, follow these steps:

1. At the left margin, type the author's last name in full, followed by a comma and a space.

2. Type the author's first initial (*not* the full first name), a period, a space, the middle initial (if available), then a period and a space.

Remember: *Never, never* use the full first name!

3. In parentheses, type the date of publication. Type a period and a space.

4. Type the article title, followed by a period and a space. Only the first word has an initial capital letter; the rest have initial lower-case letters unless they are proper names.

5. In italics, type the title of the journal, a space, the volume number, and a comma and a space.

6. Type the article number, followed by a period and a space.

7. Type the word "Retrieved," then the month, day, and year of the retrieval, followed by the word "from" and the complete URL, as shown in Figure 143.

   The URL should link directly to the article. Do not end with any punctuation that is not part of the path statement; otherwise, you may confuse the reader during the retrieval process.

8. If your reference continues to a second line, double-space the second line and indent it three spaces. If the URL goes to another line, break it after a slash or before a period.

Follow this format exactly. See Appendix F for a complete list of references.

```
Johnson, D. W. (2002, June 10). Twelve ways to motivate

   your employees. Management Today, 8, Article 5432b.

   Retrieved March 23, 2002, from http://www

   .managementtoday.com/volume8/5432b.html
```

Figure 143. Example of a Reference of an Article in a Journal Available Only on the Internet.

Referencing an Article From the Internet and Based on a Print Source

Many print journals and magazines are reproduced on the Internet. The articles are generally the same in both places. While this may change in the future, the current format for an article reviewed on the Internet but based on a print source is the same as for the print version of the article with one exception: the words [Electronic version]. A reference of such an Internet article appears as shown in Figure 144 and consists of the following elements:

- Author's last name

- Author's first initial, and middle initial, if relevant

- Year of publication

- Title of article

- Words "Electronic version"

- Title of periodical

- Volume and/or issue and page numbers

- If the article is different from the print source:

    - Date document was retrieved

    - URL

To create this reference, follow these steps:

1. At the left margin, type the author's last name in full, followed by a comma and a space.

2. Type the author's first initial (*not* the full first name), a period, a space, the middle initial (if available), then a period and a space.

Remember: *Never, never* use the full first name!

3. In parentheses, type the year of publication (or, if not available, the year of the search), followed by a period and a space.

4. Type the article title, followed by a space. Use an initial capital letter on the first word but use lower-case letters on the remaining words unless they are proper names.

5. If the article is the same as the print version, continue with this step and refer to the first example in Figure 144. If it is different, however, skip this step, refer to the second example in Figure 144, type a period and a space, and go to Step 6. In brackets, type "Electronic version," followed by a period and a space.

6. In italics, type the title of the periodical, a comma, a space, and the volume number, followed by a comma and a space.

7. Type a space, the page number(s), a period, and a space.

8. If the article is the same as the print source, your reference should look just like the first example shown in Figure 144. Skip to Step 10. If the article has been changed, however, go to Step 9, and refer to the second example in Figure 144.

9. Type the word "Retrieved," then the month, day, and year of the retrieval, followed by the word "from" and the complete URL, as shown in the second example in Figure 144.

   The URL should link directly to the article. Do not end with any punctuation that is not part of the path statement; otherwise, you may confuse the reader during the retrieval process.

10. If your reference continues to a second line, double-space the second line and indent it three spaces. If the URL goes to another line, break it after a slash or before a period.

Follow this format exactly. See Appendix F for a complete list of references.

```
Johnson, D. W. (2002). Twelve ways to motivate your

   employees [Electronic version]. Management Today, 8,

   25-26.
```

```
Johnson, D. W. (2002). Twelve ways to motivate your

   Employees. Management Today, 8, 25-26. Retrieved

   March 23, 2002, from http://www.managementtoday

   .com/Volume8/5432b.html
```

Figure 144. Example of a Reference of an Article From the Internet and Based on a Print Source.

Referencing an Article in a Journal Available Only on the Internet and Retrieved Using File Transfer Protocol (FTP)

A reference of an article obtained from a journal available only on the Internet and retrieved using FTP appears as shown in Figure 145 and consists of the following elements:

- Author's last name

- Author's first initial, and middle initial, if available

- Year of publication

- Title of article

- Title of periodical

- Volume number

- Words "Retrieved from"

- Date article was retrieved

- URL

To create this reference, follow these steps:

1. At the left margin, type the author's last name in full, followed by a comma and a space.

2. Type the author's first initial (*not* the full first name), a period, a space, the middle initial (if available), then a period and a space.

Remember: *Never, never* use the full first name!

3. In parentheses, type the date, followed by a period and a space.

4. Type the article title, followed by a period and a space. Use an initial capital letter on the first word but use lower-case letters on the remaining words unless they are proper names.

5. In italics, type the title of the journal, a comma, a space, and the volume number. Then type a period and a space.

6. Type the word "Retrieved," then the month, day, and year of the retrieval, followed by the word "from" and the complete URL, as shown in the second example in Figure 145.

The URL should link directly to the article. Do not end with any punctuation that is not part of the path statement; otherwise, you may confuse the reader during the retrieval process.

7.   If your reference continues to a second line, double-space the second line and indent it three spaces. If the URL goes to another line, break it after a slash or before a period.

Follow this format exactly. See Appendix F for a complete list of references.

```
Johnson, D. W. (1993). Twelve ways to motivate

   your employees. Management Today, 23. Retrieved

   June 20, 2002, from ftp://ftp.conraduniv.edu/

   business/management.93.4.14.motivation-employees.mt
```

Figure 145. Example of a Reference of an Article in a Journal Available Only on the Internet and Retrieved Using FTP.

Referencing an Article in a Newsletter Available Only on the Internet

A reference of an article from a newsletter available only on the Internet appears as shown in Figure 146 and consists of the following elements:

- Author's last name

- Author's first initial, and middle initial, if available

- Year (and month, if available) of publication

- Title of article

- Title of periodical

- The words "on-line serial"

- Volume and issue number, if available

- The words "Retrieved from"

- URL

To create this reference, follow these steps:

1. At the left margin, type the author's last name in full, followed by a comma and a space.

2. Type the author's first initial (*not* the full first name), a period, a space, the middle initial (if available), then a period and a space.

Remember: *Never, never* use the full first name!

3. In parentheses, type the date, followed by a period and a space.

4. Type the article title, followed by a period and a space. Only the first word of the title has an initial capital letter; the rest have initial lower-case letters unless they are proper names.

5. In italics, type the title of the journal, a comma, a space, and the volume number. Capitalize the first letter of each main word in the title.

6. Immediately after the volume number, and in parentheses, type the issue number, if available, followed by a period and a space.

7. Type the word "Retrieved," followed by the month, day, and year the article was retrieved, then "from," followed by a space and the complete URL.

8. Type the URL. It should link directly to the article. Do not end with any punctuation that is not part of the path statement; otherwise, you may confuse the reader during the retrieval process.

9. If your reference continues to a second line, double-space the second line and indent it three spaces. If the URL goes to another line, break it after a slash or before a period.

Follow this format exactly. See Appendix F for a complete list of references.

Johnson, D. W. (2000, March). Twelve ways to motivate

   your employees. *Management Today*, 4(14). Retrieved

   May 23, 2002, from http://www.managementtoday.com/

   subscribe/newsletter6.html

Figure 146. Example of a Reference of an Article From a Newsletter Available Only on the Internet.

Referencing Non-Periodical Documents on the Internet

This section shows you how to reference a:

- Multipage document created by a private organization and without a date

- Chapter or section in an Internet document

- Stand-alone document with no author or date

- Document available on a university department or program Web site

Referencing a Multipage Document Created by a Private Organization and Without a Date

A reference of a multipage document created by a private organization and without a date appears as shown in Figure 147 and consists of the following elements:

- Name of organization

- Abbreviation "n.d." for "no date"

- Title of document

- Words "Retrieved from"

- Date document was retrieved

- URL

To create this reference, follow these steps:

1. At the left margin, type the organization's name in full, followed by a period. Capitalize the first letter of all main words of the organization's name.

2. In parentheses, type the letters "n.d.," followed by a period and a space.

3. In italics, type the name of the article and follow it with a period and a space. Use an initial capital letter on the first word of the title, then lower-case letters on all remaining words unless they are proper names.

4. Type the word "Retrieved," followed by the month, day, and year the article was retrieved, then "from," followed by a space.

5. Type the complete URL. It should link directly to the article. Do not end with any punctuation that is not part of the path statement; otherwise, you may confuse the reader during the retrieval process.

NOTE: *If the document pages or sections have different URLs, list the URL that links to the document's home page.*

6. If your reference continues to a second line, double-space the second line and indent it three spaces. If the URL goes to another line, break it after a slash or before a period.

Follow this format exactly. See Appendix F for a complete list of references.

```
American Business Association. (n.d.). American

    Business Association survey--Management

    opportunities in the fortune 500 companies.

    Retrieved January 30, 2002, from http://www

    .aba.com
```

Figure 147. Example of a Reference of a Multipage Document Created by a Private Organization and Without a Date.

Referencing a Chapter or Section in an Internet Document

A reference of a chapter or section in an Internet document appears as shown in Figure 148 and consists of the following elements:

- Author's last name

- Author's first initial, and middle initial, if available

- Date of publication

- Title of chapter or section

- Word "In"

- Title of document

- Chapter or section number (not page numbers)

- Words "Retrieved from"

- Date document was retrieved

- URL

To create this reference, follow these steps:

1. At the left margin, type the author's last name in full, followed by a comma and a space.

2. Type the author's first initial (*not* the full first name), followed by a period and a space, then the middle initial (if available), followed by a period and a space. If the author's middle name is not listed, just use the first initial.

    Remember: *Never, never* use the full first name!

3. Type the date of publication in parentheses, followed by a period and a space. Include the month and day, if relevant.

4. Type the name of the article and follow it with a period and a space.

5. Type the word "In," followed by the complete title of the document in which this chapter or section appears. Italicize the title of the document. Use an initial capital letter on the first word and initial lower-case letters on the rest unless they are proper names. Follow the title with a space.

6. Type an opening parenthesis, then the abbreviation "chap." for chapter or "sec." for section, followed by a space, the chapter or section number, a closing parenthesis, a period, and a space.

7. Type the word "Retrieved," followed by a space, then the month, day, and year the article was retrieved, then "from," followed by a space.

8. Type the complete URL. It should link directly to the article. Do not end with any punctuation that is not part of the path statement; otherwise, you may confuse the reader during the retrieval process.

9. If your reference continues to a second line, double-space the second line and indent it three spaces. If the URL goes to another line, break it after a slash or before a period.

Follow this format exactly. See Appendix F for a complete list of references.

```
Johnson, D. W. (2002, February 23). Management

    opportunities in high-tech companies. In

    Career opportunities in the twenty-first

    century (chap. 4). Retrieved January 30, 2002,

    from http://www.aba.com
```

Figure 148. Example of a Reference of a Chapter or Section in an Internet Document.

Referencing a Stand-alone Document Without an Author or Date

A reference of a stand-alone document without an author or date appears as shown in Figure 149 and consists of the following elements:

- Title of document

- Abbreviation "n.d." for "no date"

- Words "Retrieved from"

- Date document was retrieved

- URL

To create this reference, follow these steps:

1. At the left margin, type the title of the document. Use an initial capital letter on the first word but use lower-case letters on the remaining words unless they are proper names. Follow the title with a period and a space.

2. In parentheses, type "n.d.," followed by a period and a space.

3. Type the word "Retrieved," followed by the date the document was retrieved from the electronic source. Type the month, the day, and the year as shown in Figure 149. Follow the date with a comma and a space.

4. Type the word "from" and the complete URL. The URL should link directly to the article.

   Do not end with any punctuation that is not part of the path statement; otherwise, you may confuse the reader during the retrieval process.

5. If your reference continues to a second line, double-space the second line and indent it three spaces. If the URL goes to another line, break it after a slash or before a period.

Follow this format exactly. See Appendix F for a complete list of references.

Current trends in hepatitis treatment. (n.d.).

Retrieved February 8, 2002, from http://www

.medreportsfile.org/hepatitis/treatment/

currenttrends.htm

Figure 149. Example of a Reference of a Stand-alone Document With No Author or Date.

Referencing a Document Available on a University Program or Department Web Site

A reference of a document available on a university program or department Web site appears as shown in Figure 150 and consists of the following elements:

- Author's last name

- Author's first initial, and middle initial, if available

- Date of publication

- Title of document

- Words "Retrieved from"

- Date document was retrieved

- Name of host organization and department or program (if Web site is complex)

- URL

To create this reference, follow these steps:

1. At the left margin, type the author's last name in full, followed by a comma and a space.

2. Type the author's first initial (*not* the full first name), followed by a period and a space, then the middle initial (if available), followed by a period and a space. If the author's middle name is not listed, just use the first initial.

   Remember: *Never, never* use the full first name!

3. Type an opening parenthesis, then the date of publication. Include the month and day, if relevant. Type a closing parenthesis, followed by a period and a space.

4. In italics, type the name of the document, followed by a period and a space.

5. Type the word "Retrieved," followed by a space, then the date the article was retrieved in month, day, year format. Follow it with a comma and a space.

6. Type the word "from," then, if the Web site is a complex one, type the name of the host organization, followed by a comma and a space, then the name of the department or program, followed by a colon.

7. Type the complete URL. The URL should link directly to the article.

    Do not end with any punctuation that is not part of the path statement; otherwise, you may confuse the reader during the retrieval process.

8. If your reference continues to a second line, double-space the second line and indent it three spaces. If the URL goes to another line, break it after a slash or before a period.

    Follow this format exactly. See Appendix F for a complete list of references.

```
Johnson, D. W. (2002). Management and technology

   in the 21st century. Retrieved January 30, 2002,

   from Evergreen University, Information Technology

   Department Web site: http://www.evergreen.edu/

   itdept/publications/articles/mantech2.html
```

Figure 150. Example of a Reference of a Document Available on a University Department or Program Web Site.

Referencing Newsgroups, Online Forums and Discussion Groups, and Electronic Mailing Lists

This section shows you how to reference a:

- Message posted to a newsgroup

- Message posted to an online forum or discussion group

- Message posted to an electronic mailing list

Be careful when referencing a message from one of these lists; ensure that it has scholarly content and will be retrievable to your readers.

NOTE: *If the message has scholarly content but you are not sure it will be retrievable in the future, cite it in the text as a personal communication (see page 68); do not include it in the reference list.*

Referencing a Message Posted to a Newsgroup

A reference of message posted to a newsgroup appears as shown in Figure 151 and consists of the following elements:

- Author's last name (or screen name, if the actual name is not available)

- Author's first initial, and middle initial, if available

- Date message was posted (year, month, and day)

- Subject line content

- Message identifier (if available)

- Words "Message posted to"

- Address of the newsgroup

To create this reference, follow these steps:

1. At the left margin, type the author's last name in full, followed by a comma and a space.

2. Type the author's first initial (*not* the full first name), a period, a space, the middle initial (if available), then a period and a space.

Remember: *Never, never* use the full first name!

> ***NOTE:*** *If the author's real name is not available, use the screen name, as shown in the second example in Figure 151.*

3. In parentheses, type date the message was posted. First type the year, followed by a comma and a space, then the month and day. Follow the closing parenthesis with a period and a space.

4. Type the subject line from the message. Use an initial capital letter on the first word but use lower-case letters on the remaining words unless they are proper names. If there is a message identifier, end with a space and go to Step 5. If there is no message identifier, end with a period and a space and go to Step 6.

5. Type an opening bracket, the message identifier, and a closing bracket, followed by a period and a space.

6. Type the words "Message posted to," followed by a space.

7. Type the complete path statement for the newsgroup. The path statement should link directly to the newsgroup.

   Do not end with any punctuation that is not part of the path statement; otherwise, you may confuse the reader during the retrieval process.

8. If your reference continues to a second line, double-space the second line and indent it three spaces. If the path statement goes to another line, break it after a slash or before a period.

Follow this format exactly. See Appendix F for a complete list of references.

```
Jones, S. L. (2002, May 14). Management trends [Msg 5].

   Message posted to news://usbusiness.trends
```

```
The boss. (2002, May 14). Management trends [Msg 5].

   Message posted to news://usbusiness.trends
```

Figure 151. Examples of a Reference of a Message Posted to a Newsgroup.

Referencing a Message Posted to an Online Forum or Discussion Group

A reference of message posted to an online forum or discussion group appears as shown in Figure 152 and consists of the following elements:

- Author's last name (or screen name, if the actual name is not available)

- Author's first initial, and middle initial, if available

- Date message was posted (year, month, and day)

- Subject line content

- Message identifier (if available)

- Words "Message posted to"

- URL

To create this reference, follow these steps:

1. At the left margin, type the author's last name in full, followed by a comma and a space.

2. Type the author's first initial (*not* the full first name), a period, a space, the middle initial (if available), then a period and a space.

Remember: *Never, never* use the full first name!

3. In parentheses, type date the message was posted. First type the year, followed by a comma and a space, then the month and day. Follow the closing parenthesis with a period and a space.

4. Type the subject line from the message. Use an initial capital letter on the first word but use lower-case letters on the remaining words unless they are proper names.

    If there is a message identifier, type a space and go to Step 5. If there is no message identifier, type a period and a space and go to Step 6.

5. Type an opening bracket, the message identifier, and a closing bracket, followed by a period and a space.

6. Type the words "Message posted to," followed by a space.

7. Type the complete URL. The URL should link directly to the article.

   Do not end with any punctuation that is not part of the path statement; otherwise, you may confuse the reader during the retrieval process.

8. If your reference continues to a second line, double-space the second line and indent it three spaces. If the URL goes to another line, break it after a slash or before a period.

Follow this format exactly. See Appendix F for a complete list of references.

```
Russell, S. A. (2002, May 14). Ideas for department

   efficiency [Msg 10]. Message posted to http://www.

   discussion.com/message/efficiency/10
```

Figure 152. Example of a Reference of a Message Posted to an Online Forum or Discussion Group.

Referencing a Message Posted to an Electronic Mailing List

A reference of message posted to an electronic mailing list appears as shown in Figure 153 and consists of the following elements:

- Author's last name

- Author's first initial, and middle initial, if available

- Date message was posted (year, month, and day)

- Subject line content

- Words "Message posted to"

- Name of mailing list

- Words "archived at"

- URL

To create this reference, follow these steps:

1. At the left margin, type the author's last name in full, followed by a comma and a space.

2. Type the author's first initial (*not* the full first name), a period, a space, the middle initial (if available), then a period and a space.

Remember: *Never, never* use the full first name!

3. In parentheses, type date the message was posted. First type the year, followed by a comma and a space, then the month and day. Follow the closing parenthesis with a period and a space.

4. Type the subject line from the message. Use an initial capital letter on the first word but use lower-case letters on the remaining words unless they are proper names. Follow the subject line with a period and a space.

5. Type the words "Message posted to," followed by a space.

6. Type the name of the electronic mailing list, followed by a comma and a space.

7. Type the words "archived at," followed by a space.

8. Type the complete URL for the archived version of the message. The URL should link directly to the archived version.

    Do not end with any punctuation that is not part of the path statement; otherwise, you may confuse the reader during the retrieval process.

9. If your reference continues to a second line, double-space the second line and indent it three spaces. If the URL goes to another line, break it after a slash or before a period.

Follow this format exactly. See Appendix F for a complete list of references.

```
Berovic, M. (2002, June 14). I have an idea. Message

   posted to SoCalWriters electronic mailing list,

   archived at http://www.socalwriters.com/mail-archive

   .socalwriters/msg00014.html
```

Figure 153. Example of a Reference of a Message Posted to an Electronic Mailing List.

Referencing Proceedings of Meetings and Symposia

This section shows you how to reference:

- Paper presented at a symposium with an abstract retrieved from a university Web site

- Paper presented at a virtual conference

Referencing a Paper Presented at a Symposium with an Abstract Retrieved From a University Web Site

A reference of paper presented at a symposium with an abstract retrieved from a university Web site appears as shown in Figure 154 and consists of the following elements:

- Author's last name

- Author's first initial, and middle initial, if available

- Date message was posted (year, month, and day)

- Title of the paper

- Words "Paper presented at the"

- Name of symposium

- Words "Abstract retrieved from"

- Date abstract was retrieved

- URL

To create this reference, follow these steps:

1. At the left margin, type the author's last name in full, followed by a comma and a space.

2. Type the author's first initial (*not* the full first name), a period, a space, the middle initial (if available), then a period and a space.

Remember: Never, never use the full first name!

3. In parentheses, type date the message was posted. First type the year, followed by a comma and a space, then the month and day. Follow the closing parenthesis with a period and a space.

4. In italics, type the title of the paper. Use an initial capital letter on the first word but use lower-case letters on the remaining words unless they are proper names. Follow the title with a period and a space.

5. Type the words "Paper presented at the," followed by a space.

6. Type the name of the symposium, followed by a period and a space.

7. Type the words "Abstract retrieved," followed by a space.

8. Type the date the abstract was retrieved in month, day, year, format, followed by a comma and a space.

9. Type the word "from," followed by a space.

10. Type the complete URL for the abstract of the paper.

     The path statement should link directly to the article. Do not end with any punctuation that is not part of the path statement; otherwise, you may confuse the reader during the retrieval process.

11. If your reference continues to a second line, double-space the second line and indent it three spaces. If the URL goes to another line, break it after a slash or before a period.

Follow this format exactly. See Appendix F for a complete list of references.

```
Berovic, V. (2001, October 23). Communication strategies

    for the new millennium. Paper presented at the 2001

    Symposium on Business Communication. Abstract

    retrieved January 14, 2002, from http://www

    .technicalcommunication.com/papers/comstrategies/
```

Figure 154. Example of a Reference of a Paper Presented at a Symposium With an Abstract Retrieved From a University Web Site.

Referencing a Paper Presented at a Virtual Conference

A reference of paper presented at a virtual conference appears as shown in Figure 155 and consists of the following elements:

- Author's last name

- Author's first initial, and middle initial, if available

- Year message was posted

- Title of the paper

- Words "Paper presented at the"

- Name of virtual conference

- Words "Retrieved from"

- Date paper was retrieved

- URL for the virtual conference

To create this reference, follow these steps:

1. At the left margin, type the author's last name in full, followed by a comma and a space.

2. Type the author's first initial (*not* the full first name), a period, a space, the middle initial (if available), then a period and a space.

Remember: *Never, never* use the full first name!

3. In parentheses, type date the message was posted. First type the year, followed by a comma and a space, then the month and day. Follow the closing parenthesis with a period and a space.

4. In italics, type the title of the paper. Use an initial capital letter on the first word but use lower-case letters on the remaining words unless they are proper names. Follow the title with a period and a space.

5. Type the words "Paper presented at the," followed by a space.

6. Type the name of the virtual conference, followed by a period and a space.

7. Type the word "Retrieved," followed by a space.

8. Type the date the paper was retrieved in month, day, year, format, followed by a comma and a space.

9. Type the word "from," followed by a space.

10. Type the complete URL for the paper.

    The URL should link directly to the article. Do not end with any punctuation that is not part of the path statement; otherwise, you may confuse the reader during the retrieval process.

11. If your reference continues to a second line, double-space the second line and indent it three spaces. If the URL goes to another line, break it after a slash or before a period.

Follow this format exactly. See Appendix F for a complete list of references.

```
Motts, D. G. (2002). Marketing strategies for today's

    international business. Paper presented at the

    2002 International Business virtual conference.

    Retrieved June 13, 2002, from http://www

    .Internationalbusinessassociation.org/2002conference/

    papers/marketingstrategies2.html
```

Figure 155. Example of a Reference of a Paper Presented at a Virtual Conference.

Referencing Technical or Research Reports

This section shows you how to reference:

- Report from a university that is available on a private organization's Web site

- U.S. government report available on a government agency Web site and with no publication date

- Report from a private organization that is available on the organization's Web site

- Abstract of a technical report retrieved from a university Web site

Referencing a Report From a University Available on a Private Organization's Web Site

A reference of a report from a university available on a private organization's Web site appears as shown in Figure 156 and consists of the following elements:

- University's name

- Institute or department name

- Date of publication

- Title of document

- Words "Retrieved from"

- Date document was retrieved from the Web site

- Name of host organization's Web site

- URL

To create this reference, follow these steps:

1. At the left margin, type the author's last name in full, followed by a comma and a space.

2. Type the author's first initial (*not* the full first name), followed by a period and a space, then the middle initial (if available), followed by a period and a space. If the author's middle name is not listed, just use the first initial.

Remember: *Never, never* use the full first name!

3. In parentheses, type the date of publication. Include the month and day, if relevant. Followed the date with a period and a space.

4. In italics, type the name of the report, then follow it with a period and a space.

5. Type the word "Retrieved," followed by the date the article was retrieved in month, day, year format. Follow it with a comma and a space.

6. Type the word "from," then, if the host organization is different from the author, type the name of the host organization's Web site, followed by a colon and a space.

7. Type the complete URL. The URL should link directly to the article. Do not end with any punctuation that is not part of the path statement; otherwise, you may confuse the reader during the retrieval process.

8. If your reference continues to a second line, double-space the second line and indent it three spaces. If the URL goes to another line, break it after a slash or before a period.

Follow this format exactly. See Appendix F for a complete list of references.

```
University of the West, San Diego, Institute for

    Neonatal Medicine. (2002, February). Diagnostic

    techniques for neonatal specialists. Retrieved

    March 23, 2002, from The Beckman Institute Web

    site: http://www.Beckmaninstitute.org/publications/

    articles/neonatal4.html
```

Figure 156. Example of a Reference of a Report from a University That is Available on a Private Organization Web Site.

Referencing a U.S. Government Report Available on a Government Agency Web Site and Without a Publication Date

A reference of a U.S. Government report available on a government agency Web site and without a publication date appears as shown in Figure 157 and consists of the following elements:

- Agency's name
- Letters "n.d."
- Title of report
- Words "Retrieved from"
- Date document was retrieved from the Web site
- URL

To create this reference, follow these steps:

1. At the left margin, type the agency's name in full, followed by a period and a space.

2. In parentheses, type the letters "n.d.," followed by period and a space.

3. In italics, type the name of the report, and follow it with a period and a space.

4. Type the word "Retrieved," followed by the date the article was retrieved in month, day, year format. Follow the date with a comma and a space.

5. Type the word "from," Type the complete URL. The URL should link directly to the article. Do not end with any punctuation that is not part of the path statement; otherwise, you may confuse the reader during the retrieval process.

6. If your reference continues to a second line, double-space the second line and indent it three spaces. If the URL goes to another line, break it after a slash or before a period.

    Follow this format exactly. See Appendix F for a complete list of references.

Interagency Arctic Research Policy Committee. (n.d.).

United States Arctic Research Plan. Retrieved

June 3, 2002, from http://www.nasa.org/

publications/artic/usarp.html

*Figure 157. Example of a Reference of a U.S. Government Report
Available on a Government Agency Web Site and Without
a Date.*

Referencing a Report From a Private Organization and Available on the Organization's Web Site

A reference of a report from a private organization and available on the organization's Web site appears as shown in Figure 158 and consists of the following elements:

- Private organization's name

- Date of publication

- Title of document

- Words "Retrieved from"

- Date document was retrieved from the Web site

- URL

To create this reference, follow these steps:

1. At the left margin, type the organization's name in full, followed by a period and a space.

2. In parentheses, type the date of publication, followed by a period and a space. Include the month and day, if relevant.

3. In italics, type the name of the report and follow it with a period and a space.

4. Type the word "Retrieved," followed by the date the article was retrieved in month, day, year format. Follow the date with a comma and a space.

5. Type the word "from," a space, then the complete URL. The URL should link directly to the report.

   Do not end with any punctuation that is not part of the path statement; otherwise, you may confuse the reader during the retrieval process.

6. If your reference continues to a second line, double-space the second line and indent it three spaces. If the URL goes to another line, break it after a slash or before a period.

Follow this format exactly. See Appendix F for a complete list of references.

```
Corona Space Society. (2002). Increasing public

    interest in the space program. Retrieved July 3,

    2002, from http://www.css.org/articles/public

    interest/publicinterest.doc
```

Figure 158. Example of a Reference of a Report From a Private Organization That is Available on the Organization's Web Site.

Referencing an Abstract of a Technical Report Retrieved from a University Web Site

A reference of an abstract of a technical report retrieved from a university Web site appears as shown in Figure 159 and consists of the following elements:

- Author's last name

- Author's first initial, and middle initial, if available

- Date of publication

- Title of document

- Report number, if relevant

- Words "Abstract retrieved from"

- Date document was retrieved from the Web site

- URL

To create this reference, follow these steps:

1. At the left margin, type the author's last name in full, followed by a comma and a space.

2. Type the author's first initial (*not* the full first name), followed by a period and a space, then the middle initial (if available), followed by a period and a space. If the author's middle name is not listed, just use the first initial.

   Remember: *Never, never* use the full first name!

3. In parentheses, type the date of publication, Include the month and day, if relevant. Follow the date with a period and a space.

4. In italics, type the name of the report, then follow it with a a space.

   NOTE: If the report has a series name and number, include it in brackets as shown in the second example in Figure 159.

5. In parentheses, type the series title and report number in full. Follow it these items with a period and a space.

6. Type the words "Abstract retrieved," followed by the date the article was retrieved in month, day, year format. Follow the date with a comma and a space.

7. Type the word "from," then the complete URL. The URL should link directly to the report.

   Do not end with any punctuation that is not part of the path statement; otherwise, you may confuse the reader during the retrieval process.

8. If your reference continues to a second line, double-space the second line and indent it three spaces. If the URL goes to another line, break it after a slash or before a period.

   Follow this format exactly. See Appendix F for a complete list of references.

```
Johnson, D. W. (2002). Diagnostic techniques for

   neonatal specialists (Canyon University Pediatric

   Research Report No. 5). Abstract retrieved March

   23, 2002, from http://www.canyonuniversity.edu/

   publications/articles/neonatal.html
```

Figure 159. Example of a Reference of an Abstract of a Technical Report Retrieved From a University Web Site.

Referencing Computer Products

You can reference four types of computer materials:

- Software

- Programs

- Programming languages

- Manuals

You do not need to include standard off-the-shelf programs such as Microsoft Office (Word, Excel, PowerPoint, Access, FrontPage, etc.), Adobe Illustrator or Photoshop, Quickbooks Pro, etc., in the reference list. Just mention them by name and version number in the text of your document. The same is true for specialized software or computer programs with limited distribution.

Referencing Computer Software, Programs, and Programming Languages

A reference of computer software, a program, or a programming language appears as shown in Figure 160. The format for referencing these three items is the same; therefore, only the example for computer software is shown. This software program has an author and the example consists of the following elements:

- Author's last name

- Author's first initial, and middle initial, if available

- Year of copyright

- Title of software

- Word "Version"

- Version number, if applicable

- Words "Computer software"

NOTE: *If this is a computer program or programming language, use the words "Computer program," or "Computer programming language."*

- City where the program, software, or programming language publisher or producer is located

- Publisher's or producer's name

To create this reference, follow these steps:

1. At the left margin, type the author's last name in full, followed by a comma and a space.

2. Type the author's first initial (*not* the full first name), a period, a space, the middle initial (if available), then a period and a space.

Remember: *Never, never* use the full first name!

3. In parentheses, type the copyright year of this software. Follow it with a period and a space.

4. Type the software title. Use an initial capital letter on the first word but use lower-case letters on the remaining words unless they are proper names, followed by a space.

5. In parentheses, type the word "Version," followed by the version number and a space.

6. In brackets, type the words "Computer software," followed by a period and a space.

7. Type the city where the producer is located (and the two-letter state code, if the city is not listed in Table 15), followed by a colon and a space.

8. Type the publisher or producer's name. If it is the author(s), type the word "Author" or "Authors" here. End with a period.

9. If your reference continues to a second line, double-space the second line and indent it three spaces.

Follow this format exactly. See Appendix F for a complete list of references.

```
Rodriguez, J. T. (1993). The resume builder (Version

   2.0) [Computer software]. Santa Clara, CA: Business

   Builders, Inc.
```

Figure 160. Example of a Reference of Computer Software With An Author.

Referencing a Computer Software Program and Manual Available on a University Web Site

A reference of a computer software program with a manual and available on a university Web site appears as shown in Figure 161. This software program has an author and the example consists of the following elements:

- Author's last name

- Author's first initial, and middle initial, if available

- Year of copyright

- Title of software

- Words "Computer software and manual"

- Words "Retrieved from"

- URL

To create this reference, follow these steps:

1. At the left margin, type the author's last name in full, followed by a comma and a space.

2. Type the author's first initial (*not* the full first name), a period, a space, the middle initial (if available), then a period and a space.

Remember: *Never, never* use the full first name!

3. In parentheses, type the copyright year of this software. End with a period and a space.

4. Type the software title, followed by a space. Use an initial capital letter on the first word but use lower-case letters on the remaining words unless they are proper names.

5. In brackets, type the words "Computer software and manual," followed by a period and a space.

6. Type the words "Retrieved from," then the complete URL. The URL should link directly to the software program and manual.

    Do not end with any punctuation that is not part of the path statement; otherwise, you may confuse the reader during the retrieval process.

7.   If your reference continues to a second line, double-space the
     second line and indent it three spaces. If the URL goes to
     another line, break it after a slash or before a period.

Follow this format exactly. See Appendix F for a complete list of
references.

```
Maruyama, T. L. (2001). Lexus 300 dimensions 2002

    [Computer software and manual]. Retrieved from

    http://www.gmac.com/publications/products/

    software/lexus300.htm
```

*Figure 161. Example of a Reference of Computer Software and Manual
Available on a University Web Site.*

Referencing Raw Data

Raw data is data that has been gathered but not analyzed. This section shows you how to reference a:

- Data file available from a government agency

- Data file available from the National Technical Information Service (NTIS) Web site

Referencing a Data File Available from a Government Agency

A reference of a data file that is available from a government agency appears as shown in Figure 162 and consists of the following elements:

- Title of data file

- Version number, if applicable

- Words "Data file"

- Location of agency from which this data file is available

- Name of the agency from which this data file is available

To create this reference, follow these steps:

1. At the left margin, in italics, type the data file title, followed by a space.

2. In parentheses, not italicized, type the version number, followed by a space.

3. In brackets, type the words "Data file," followed by a period and a space.

4. Type the city (and state, if needed) where the government agency is located, followed by a colon and a space.

5. Type the name of the government agency, followed by a period.

6. If your reference continues to a second line, double-space the second line and indent it three spaces.

Follow this format exactly. See Appendix F for a complete list of references.

American Business Association survey--Management

opportunities in the fortune 500 companies

(Version 7) [Data file]. Washington, DC: Small

Business Administration.

Figure 162. Example of a Reference of a Data File That is Available From a Government Agency.

Referencing a Data File Available From the National Technical Information Service (NTIS) Web Site

A reference of a data file available from the National Technical Information Service (NTIS) Web site appears in Figure 163 and consists of the following elements:

- Authoring agency's name(s)

- Year report was copyrighted

- Title of report

- Number of report, if relevant

- Words "Data file"

- Words "Available from"

- Name of Web site

- URL

To create this reference, follow these steps:

1. At the left margin, type the name of the authoring agency, followed by a period and a space.

2. In parentheses, type the copyright year, followed by a period and a space.

3. In italics, type the report title. Use an initial capital letter on the first word but use lower-case letters on the remaining words unless they are proper names. Follow the title with a space.

4. In brackets, type the words "Data file." Do not italicize these words or the brackets. End with a period and a space.

5. Type the words "Available from" (to indicate that the URL leads to information on how to get the cited material, not to the material itself), then the name of the Web site, followed by a comma and a space.

6. Type the complete URL. The URL should link directly to the software program and manual.

7. If your reference continues to a second line, double-space the second line and begin it back at the left margin. If the URL goes to a second line, break it after a slash or before a period.

Follow this format exactly. See Appendix F for a complete list of references.

Department of Infant Services, World Health

    Organization. (2001). *Infant health problems in*

    West Africa, 2001 [Data file]. Available from

    National Technical Information Service Web site,

    http://www.ntis.gov

Figure 163. Example of a Data File From the National Technical Information Service (NTIS) Web Site.

Referencing Aggregated Databases

This section shows you how to reference a(n):

- Electronic copy of a journal article retrieved from a database

- Daily newspaper article, electronic version available by search

- Electronic copy of an abstract obtained from a secondary database

- Electronic copy of a U.S. government report available by search from the GPO Access database on the Web

Referencing an Electronic Copy of a Journal Article Retrieved From a Database

A reference of a journal article retrieved from a database appears as shown in Figure 164 and consists of the following elements:

- Author's last name

- Author's first initial, and middle initial, if available

- Year of journal issue

- Title of article

- Title of journal

- Volume (and issue) number, if available

- Page number(s) of article

- Words "Retrieved from"

- Date article was retrieved

- Name of the database

To create this reference, follow these steps:

1. At the left margin, type the author's last name in full, followed by a comma and a space.

2. Type the author's first initial (*not* the full first name), followed by a period and a space, then the middle initial (if available), followed by a period and a space. If the author's middle name is not listed, just use the first initial.

Remember: *Never, never* use the full first name!

3. In parentheses, type the copyright year, followed by a period and a space.

4. Type the title of the article in plain type. Use an initial capital letter on the first word but use lower-case letters on the remaining words unless they are proper names. End with a period and a space.

5. Type the journal title. Use initial capital letters on all main words and follow the title with a comma, a space, and the volume number, if available. Italicize the title and the volume number. (If the issue number is available, place it in parentheses and follow it with a comma, as shown).

6. Type a space and the page numbers, followed by a period and a space.

NOTE: *Notice that the "pp." is not included in the page number shown in Figure 164. The "p." or "pp." is not used when the volume number is included.*

7. Type the word "Retrieved," followed by the date (in month, day, year format) you retrieved the article from the database. Type a comma and a space.

8. Type the word "from" followed by a space and the name of the database from which you retrieved the article. End with a period.

9. If your reference continues to a second line, double-space the second line and indent it three spaces.

Follow this format exactly. See Appendix F for a complete list of references.

```
Matthews, Y. A. (1993). Electronic communication in

    large organizations. Technical Communication, 39(2),

    60-65. Retrieved June 22, 2002, from Business Today

    database.
```

Figure 164. Example of a Reference of an Electronic Copy of a Journal Article Retrieved from a Database.

Referencing a Daily Newspaper Article, Electronic Version Available by Search

Reference a newspaper article with an author just as you would a magazine article with an author. Just put the newspaper's name where the magazine title goes. A reference for a newspaper article appears as shown in Figure 165 and consists of the following elements:

- Author's last name

- Author's first initial, and middle initial, if available

- Date of newspaper issue in year, month, day format

- Title of article

- Title of newspaper

- Words "Retrieved from"

- Date article was retrieved

- URL

To create this reference, follow these steps:

1. At the left margin, type the author's last name in full, followed by a comma and a space.

2. Type the author's first initial (*not* the full first name), followed by a period and a space, then the middle initial (if available), followed by a period and a space. If the author's middle name is not listed, just use the first initial.

Remember: *Never, never* use the full first name!

3. In parentheses, type the copyright year, followed by a comma, a space, the month of publication (the day, too, if applicable; i.e., June 15), and then a period and a space.

4. Type the title of the article in plain type. Use an initial capital letter on the first word but use lower-case letters on all the remaining words unless they are proper names. Follow the title with a period and a space. (If the title ends with a question mark, as shown in Figure 165, or an exclamation point, do not use a period.)

5. In italics, type the newspaper title. Use initial capital letters on all main words, and follow it with a comma and a space.

6. Type the word "Retrieved," followed by the date (in month, day, year format) you retrieved the article. Type a comma and a space.

7. Type the word "from" followed by a space and the complete URL. The URL should link directly to the article.

   Do not end with any punctuation that is not part of the path statement; otherwise, you may confuse the reader during the retrieval process.

8. If your reference continues to a second line, double-space the second line and indent it three spaces. If the URL goes to another line, break it after a slash or before a period.

   Follow this format exactly. See Appendix F for a complete list of references.

```
Jones, J. T. (1993, December 10). Is an upturn in

   California's economy still years away? Los Angeles

   Times. Retrieved July 13, 2002, from http://www

   .latimes.com
```

Figure 165. Example of a Reference of a Daily Newspaper Article, Electronic Version Available by Search.

Referencing an Electronic Copy of An Abstract Obtained From a Secondary Database

A reference of an electronic copy of an abstract obtained from a secondary database (one other than that for the journal archives themselves) appears as shown in Figure 166 and consists of the following elements:

- Author's last name

- Author's first initial, and middle initial, if available

- Date paper was published or presented

- Title of abstract

- Title of journal in which the abstract appeared

- Volume (and issue) number, if available

- Page number(s)

- Words "Abstract retrieved"

- Date abstract was retrieved

- Name of database

To create this reference, follow these steps:

1. At the left margin, type the author's last name in full, followed by a comma and a space.

2. Type the author's first initial (*not* the full first name), followed by a period and a space, then the middle initial (if available), followed by a period and a space. If the author's middle name is not listed, just use the first initial.

Remember: *Never, never* use the full first name!

3. In parentheses, type the date the paper was published or presented, followed by a comma, a space, the month of publication (the day, too, if applicable; i.e., June 15), and then a period and a space.

4. Type the title of the article in plain type. Use an initial capital letter on the first word but use lower-case letters on all the remaining words unless they are proper names. End the title

with a period and a space. (If the title ends with a question mark, as shown in Figure 166, or an exclamation point, do not use a period.)

5. In italics, type the journal title, followed by a comma and a space. Use initial capital letters on all main words of the title.

6. If the volume number is available, in italics, type the number only, followed by a comma and a space.

7. Type the page number(s), followed by a period and a space.

NOTE: *Notice that the "pp." is not included in the page number shown in Figure 166. The "p." or "pp." is not used when the volume number is included.*

8. Type the words "Abstract retrieved," followed by the date you retrieved the article from the database. Type a comma and a space.

9. Type the name of the database from which you retrieved the abstract. End with a period.

10. If your reference continues to a second line, double-space the second line and indent it three spaces.

Follow this format exactly. See Appendix F for a complete list of references.

```
Matthews, Y. A. (2001, December 10). Electronic

   communication in large organizations. Technical

   Communication, 39, 60-65. Abstract retrieved July

   13, 2002, from BusINFO database.
```

Figure 166. Example of a Reference of a Daily Newspaper Article, Electronic Version Available by Search.

Referencing an Electronic Copy of a U.S. Government Report Available by Search From the GPO Access Database on the Web

The Government Printing Office (GPO) prints all the publications from federal agencies. Many are available free or at a low-cost on the GPO Access database, and you may find these helpful in your research. A reference of an electronic copy of a U.S. government report available by searching the GPO Access database on the Web appears in Figure 167 and consists of the following elements:

- Issuing agency's name

- Year (and month, if relevant) report was copyrighted

- Title of report

- Number of report, if relevant

- Words "Retrieved from"

- Date report was retrieved

- Name of agency's database

- Words "via GPO Access"

- URL

To create this reference, follow these steps:

1. At the left margin, type the issuing agency's name in full, followed by a period and a space.

2. In parentheses, type the copyright year, followed by a period and a space. (Include the month, if relevant.)

3. In italics, type the report title. Only the first word has an initial capital letter; the rest of the words have initial lower-case letters unless they are proper names. Follow the title with a space.

4. In parentheses, type the publication number. Abbreviate the word "number" as "No.," followed by a period. After the closing parenthesis, type a period and a space.

5. Type the word "Retrieved," then the date the report was retrieved. Follow the date with a comma and a space.

6. Type the word "from," followed by the agency's database name and a space.

7. Type the words "via GPO Access," followed by a colon and a space.

8. Type the complete URL. It should link directly to the report.

   Do not end with any punctuation that is not part of the path statement; otherwise, you may confuse the reader during the retrieval process.

9. If your reference continues to a second line, double-space the second line and indent it three spaces.

   Follow this format exactly. See Appendix F for a complete list of references.

```
Small Business Administration. (1976). Checklist for

    going into business (Small Marketers Aid No. 71).

    Retrieved March 14, 2002, from Small Business

    Administration Reports Online via GPO Access:

    http://www.access.gpo.gov/sba_docs/marketing/sma71

    .html
```

Figure 167. Example of a Reference of an Electronic Copy of a U.S. Government Report Available by Search From the GPO Access Database on the Web.

Alphabetizing References

To alphabetize references, follow the rules in Table 18.

Table 17. Rules for Alphabetizing References in the Reference List.

RULE	EXAMPLES
1. List names in alphabetical order by last name of the first author	Gold, T. M. Golding, S. A.
2. Alphabetize the prefixes M', Mc, and Mac literally	MacIntyre McGill M'Connell
3. Alphabetize last names containing articles and prepositions by the rules of the language of origin. Refer to the biographical section of *Webster's Collegiate Dictionary* for detailed help.	Aldenbruck, B. von D'Angelo, T. L. de la Salandra, M. G. De Santos, C. R. DuBois, J. J. Van Handel, S. L. Von Richtofen, P. D.
4. Alphabetize references beginning with numbers as if the numbers were spelled out.	5 Rules for Good Management. (1994). Forbes, M. T. (1993).
5. Alphabetize multiple works by the same author(s) by year of publication, the earliest first.	Garrison, J. T. (1989). Garrison, J. T. (1994). Jansen, L. M. & Chung, H. L. (1991). Jansen, L. M. & Chung, H. L. (1993).
6. Alphabetize one-author works before multiple author works with that same author.	Garrison, J. T. (1994) Garrison, J. T. & Taylor, B. R. (1992).
7. Alphabetize works with the same first author and different second or third authors by the name of the second (then third) author.	Garrison, J. T. & Marcos, L. N. (1993). Garrison, J. T. & Taylor, B. R. (1992). Garrison, J. T., Taylor, B. R. & Javier, S. A. (1993).
8. Alphabetize works by the same author(s) with the same publication date by the title (do not count "A" or "The") and place "a," "b," etc., after the publication date.	Campbell, M. R. (1992a). The ethics of management. Campbell, M. R. (1992b). The theory of TQM.
9. Alphabetize works by different first authors with the same last name by the first initial. Include the author's initials in the text citation.	Berovic, M. (1993). Berovic, V. (1991).
10. Alphabetize works with group authors or no authors by the first significant word of the name or of the title, if no name is listed. Treat legal references likewise. If the work is listed as Anonymous, place this word, spelled completely out, as the author, and listed alphabetically in the "A" listings.	Anonymous. (2001). Grayson Consulting Group. (2000). *Helping the underprivileged.* (2002). Space Memorial Bill. (1986).

Chapter 8

Punctuation and Spelling

The APA uses punctuation rules derived from *Words into Type* (Skillin & Gay, 1974) and the *Chicago Manual of Style* (University of Chicago, 1993). For information on punctuation not shown in in this chapter, please consult these books.

This chapter explains the APA requirements of:

- commas, quotation marks, brackets, and slashes

- spelling

- numbering volumes in the reference list

Punctuation Requirements and Exceptions

Table 18 shows the punctuation requirements; Table 19 shows the exceptions to those requirements.

Table 18. APA Punctuation Requirements.

PUNCTUATION	WHERE USED	EXAMPLE
Comma	Between elements in a series of three or more items	. . .two managers, three employees, and five clients.
Double quotation marks	To introduce a word or phrase used as an ironic comment, slang, or as an invented or coined expression.	People incorrectly use the term "xerox" to mean "photocopy," as in "He xeroxed two copies of the contract."
	To set off the title of an article or chapter in a magazine or book when mentioned in the text.	Smith's (1992) article, "The Paperless Office," focuses on the use of . . . .
Brackets	To enclose parenthetical material within parentheses; use commas, if possible.	(See Appendix B [Figure B-3] for the sales figures for March, 2002.

Table 19. Punctuation Exceptions.

PUNCTUATION	DO NOT USE	TYPE AS
Comma	to separate parts of measurement	6 years 4 months
Slash	in these phrases: and/or pretest/posttest	Monday, Tuesday, or both pretest and posttest

Spelling Requirements

Table 20 shows the spelling requirements of the APA style for creating plurals of the words shown.

Table 20. Spelling Requirements.

SINGULAR	PLURAL	SINGULAR	PLURAL
appendix	appendixes	matrix	matrices
datum	data	phenomenon	phenomena

Numbering Requirements

Table 21 shows the numbering requirements when listing a volume in the references. Note that you must use an Arabic numeral, not a Roman numeral.

Table 21. Numbering Requirements.

EXAMPLE	APA STYLE REQUIREMENT
Vol. IV	Vol. 4

References

American Psychological Association. (2001). *Publication Manual of the American Psychological Association* (5th ed.). Washington, DC: Author.

Harvard Law Review Association. (2000). *The Bluebook: A Uniform System of Citation* (17th ed.). Cambridge, MA: Author.

Appendix A

Sample Report With One Heading Level

NOTE: *The example presented in this appendix is meant for viewing of heading levels only. The length of each section as shown here is not an indication of the length that your sections should be; these sections are abbreviated due to space limitations.*

NOTE: *If you are including a title page on your report, leave the title off the first page of the actual report.*

Marketing Strategies to Increase Revenue

in Acme Widgets' European Territory

Lorem ipsum dolor sit amet, consectetuer adipiscing elit, sed diam nonummy nibh euismod tin cidunt ut laoreet dolore magna aliquam erat volutpat. Ut wisi enim ad minim veniam, quis nostrud exerci tation ullamcorper suscipit lobortis nisl ut aliquip ex ea commodo consequat.

Findings

Lorem ipsum dolor sit amet, consectetuer adipiscing elit, sed diam nonummy nibh euismod tin cidunt ut laoreet dolore magna aliquam erat volutpat. Ut wisi enim ad minim veniam, quis nostrud exerci tation ullamcorper suscipit lobortis nisl ut aliquip ex ea commodo consequat.

Duis atem vel eum iriure dolor in hendrerit in vulputate velit esse molestie consequat, vel illum dolore eu feugiat nulla facilisis at vero eros et accumsan et iusto odio dignissim qui blandit praesent luptatum zzril delenit augue duis dolore te feugait nulla facilisi.

Conclusion and Recommendations

Duis atem vel eum iriure dolor in hendrerit in vulputate velit esse molestie consequat, vel illum dolore eu feugiat nulla facilisis at vero eros et accumsan et iusto odio dignissim qui blandit praesent luptatum zzril delenit augue duis dolore te.

Appendix B

Sample Report With
Two Heading Levels

NOTE: *The example presented in this appendix is meant for viewing of heading levels only. The length of each section as shown here is not an indication of the length that your sections should be; these sections are abbreviated due to space limitations.*

NOTE: *If you are including a title page on your report, leave the title off the first page of the actual report.*

Marketing Strategies to Increase Revenue

in Acme Widgets' European Territory

Lorem ipsum dolor sit amet, consectetuer adipiscing elit, sed diam nonummy nibh euismod tin cidunt ut laoreet dolore magna aliquam erat volutpat. Ut wisi enim ad minim veniam, quis nostrud exerci tation ullamcorper suscipit lobortis nisl ut aliquip ex ea commodo consequat.

Vel Illum Dolore

Lorem ipsum dolor sit amet, consectetuer adipiscing elit, sed diam nonummy nibh euismod tin cidunt ut laoreet dolore magna aliquam erat volutpat. Ut wisi enim ad minim veniam, quis nostrud exerci tation ullamcorper suscipit lobortis nisl ut aliquip ex ea commodo consequat.

Duis atem vel eum iriure dolor in hendrerit in vulputate velit esse molestie consequat, vel illum dolore eu feugiat nulla facilisis. At vero eros et accumsan et iusto odio dignissim qui blandit praesent luptatum zzril delenit augue duis dolore te feugait nulla facilisi.

Feugiat Nulla Facilisis at Vero Eros et Accumsan et Iusto Odio Dignissim Qui Blandit

Lorem ipsum dolor sit amet, consectetuer adipiscing elit, sed diam nonummy nibh euismod tin cidunt ut laoreet dolore magna aliquam erat volutpat. Ut wisi enim ad minim veniam, quis nostrud exerci tation ullamcorper suscipit lobortis nisl ut

aliquip ex ea commodo consequat. Odio dignissim qui blandit nam liber tempor cum soluta nobis.

Nostrud Exerci Tation Ullamcorper

Lorem ipsum dolor sit amet, consectetuer adipiscing elit, sed diam nonummy nibh euismod tin cidunt ut laoreet dolore magna aliquam erat volutpat. Ut wisi enim ad minim veniam, quis nostrud exerci tation ullamcorper suscipit lobortis nisl ut aliquip ex ea commodo consequat.

Nonummy Nibh Euismod

Duis atem vel eum iriure dolor in hendrerit in vulputate velit esse molestie consequat, vel illum dolore eu feugiat nulla facilisis at vero eros et accumsan et iusto odio dignissim qui blandit praesent luptatum zzril delenit augue duis dolore te feugait nulla facilisi. Nam liber tempor cum soluta nobis eleifend option congue nihil imperdiet doming id quod mazim placerat facer possim assum:

Conclusion

Ut wisi enim ad minim veniam, quis nostrud exerci tation ullamcorper suscipit lobortis nisl ut aliquip ex ea commodo consequat. Duis atem vel eum iriure dolor in hendrerit in vulputate velit esse molestie consequat, vel illum dolore eu feugiat nulla facilisis at vero eros et accumsan et iusto odio dignissim qui blandit praesent.

Appendix C

Sample Report With Three Heading Levels

NOTE: *The example presented in this appendix is meant for viewing of heading levels only. The length of each section as shown here is not an indication of the length that your sections should be; these sections are abbreviated due to space limitations.*

NOTE: *If you are including a title page on your report, leave the title off the first page of the actual report.*

Pros and Cons of Electronic Communication

at Two Large Companies

Consectetuer adipiscing elit, sed diam nonummy nibh euismod tin cidunt ut laoreet dolore magna aliquam erat volutpat. Ut wisi enim ad minim veniam, quis nostrud exerci tation.

Types of Electronic Communication at Company A

Lorem ipsum dolor sit amet, consectetuer adipiscing elit, sed diam nonummy nibh euismod tin cidunt ut laoreet. Ut wisi enim ad minim veniam, quis nostrud exerci tation.

E-mail

Lorem ipsum dolor sit amet, consectetuer adipiscing elit, sed diam nonummy nibh. Euismod tin cidunt ut laoreet dolore magna aliquam erat volutpat.

Pagers

Lorem ipsum dolor sit amet, consectetuer adipiscing elit, sed diam nonummy nibh euismod tin cidunt ut laoreet dolore magna aliquam erat volutpat. Ut wisi enim ad minim veniam, quis nostrud exerci tation.

Cell Phones

At vero eros et accumsan et iusto odio dignissim qui blandit praesent luptatum zzril delenit augue duis dolore te feugait.

Company-owned. Duis atem vel eum iriure dolor in hendrerit in vulputate velit esse molestie consequat. Vel illum dolore eu feugiat nulla facilisis at vero eros et accumsan et iusto odio.

Ut wisi enim ad minim veniam, quis nostrud exerci tation ullam corper suscipit lobortis nisl ut aliquip ex ea.

    Employee-owned. At vero eros et accumsan et iusto odio dignissim qui blandit praesent luptatum zzril delenit augue duis dolore te feugait. Qui blandit praesent luptatum zzril delenit augue duis dolore te feugait.

Fax Machines

    Vel eum iriure dolor in hendrerit in vulputate velit esse molestie consequat, vel illum dolore eu feugiat nulla facilisis. At vero eros et accumsan et iusto odio dignissim qui blandit praesent luptatum zzril delenit augue duis dolore te feugait.

    Types of Electronic Communication at Company B

    Ut wisi enim ad minim veniam, quis nostrud exerci tation ullamcorper. Suscipit lobortis nisl ut aliquip ex ea commodo consequat.

E-mail

    Duis atem vel eum iriure dolor in hendrerit in vulputate velit esse molestie consequat. Nam liber tempor cum soluta nobis eleifend option congue nihil imperdiet doming id quod mazim placerat facer possim assum.

Pagers

    Velit esse molestie consequat. Nam liber tempor cum soluta nobis eleifend option congue nihil imperdiet doming id quod mazim placerat facer possim assum.

Cell Phones

Vel illum dolore eu feugiat nulla facilisis at vero eros et accumsan et iusto odio dignissim qui blandit.

Company-owned. Atem vel eum iriure dolor in hendrerit in vulputate velit esse molestie consequat. Vel illum dolore eu feugiat nulla facilisis at vero eros et accumsan et iusto odio dignissim qui blandit praesent luptatum zzril delenit.

Employee-owned. Vulputate velit esse molestie consequat. Vel illum dolore eu feugiat nulla facilisis at vero eros et accumsan et iusto odio dignissim qui blandit praesent luptatum zzril delenit.

Fax Machines

Esse molestie consequat, vel illum dolore eu feugiat nulla facilisis at vero eros et accumsan et iusto. Odio dignissim qui blandit praesent luptatum zzril delenit augue duis dolore te feugait nulla facilisi.

Conclusion

Duis atem vel eum iriure dolor in hendrerit in vulputate velit esse molestie consequat, vel illum dolore eu feugiat nulla facilisis at vero eros et accumsan et iusto odio dignissim qui blandit praesent luptatum zzril delenit augue duis dolore te feugait nulla facilisi.

Appendix D

Sample Report With Four Heading Levels

***NOTE*:** *The example presented in this appendix is meant for viewing of heading levels only. The length of each section as shown here is not an indication of the length that your sections should be; these sections are abbreviated due to space limitations.*

***NOTE*:** *If you are including a title page on your report, leave the title off the first page of the actual report.*

Types of Cell Phones and Pagers

at Two Large Companies

Consectetuer adipiscing elit, sed diam nonummy nibh euismod tin cidunt ut laoreet dolore magna aliquam erat volutpat. Ut wisi enim ad minim veniam, quis nostrud exerci tation.

Types of Cell Phones and Pagers at Company A

Cell Phones

Lorem ipsum dolor sit amet, consectetuer adipiscing elit, sed diam nonummy nibh euismod tin cidunt ut laoreet. Ut wisi enim ad minim veniam, quis nostrud exerci tation.

Company-owned

Lorem ipsum dolor sit amet, consectetuer adipiscing elit, sed diam nonummy nibh euismod tin cidunt ut laoreet dolore magna aliquam erat volutpat.

Sprint. Ipsum dolor sit amet, consectetuer adipiscing elit. Sed diam nonummy nibh euismod tin cidunt ut laoreet dolore magna aliquam erat volutpat.

AT&T. Nonummy nibh euismod tin cidunt ut laoreet dolore magna aliquam erat volutpat. Ut wisi enim ad minim veniam, quis nostrud exerci tation.

Employee-owned

Lorem ipsum dolor sit amet, consectetuer adipiscing elit, sed diam nonummy nibh euismod tin cidunt ut laoreet dolore magna

aliquam erat volutpat. Ut wisi enim ad minim veniam, quis nostrud exerci tation.

Sprint. Ipsum dolor sit amet, consectetuer adipiscing elit. Sed diam nonummy nibh euismod tin cidunt ut laoreet dolore magna aliquam erat volutpat.

AT&T. Nonummy nibh euismod tin cidunt ut laoreet dolore magna aliquam erat volutpat. Ut wisi enim ad minim veniam, quis nostrud exerci tation.

Other brands. Ipsum dolor sit amet, consectetuer adipiscing elit. Sed diam nonummy nibh euismod tin cidunt ut laoreet dolore magna aliquam erat volutpat.

Pagers

At vero eros et accumsan et iusto odio dignissim qui blandit praesent luptatum zzril delenit augue feugait. Consectetuer adipiscing elit, sed diam nonummy.

Types of Cell Phones and Pagers at Company B

Cell Phones

Lorem ipsum dolor sit amet, consectetuer adipiscing elit, sed diam nonummy nibh euismod tin cidunt ut laoreet. Ut wisi enim ad minim veniam, quis nostrud exerci tation.

Company-owned

Lorem ipsum dolor sit amet, consectetuer adipiscing elit, sed diam nonummy nibh euismod tin cidunt ut laoreet dolore magna aliquam erat volutpat.

Sprint. Ipsum dolor sit amet, consectetuer adipiscing elit. Sed diam nonummy nibh euismod tin cidunt ut laoreet dolore magna aliquam erat volutpat.

AT&T. Nonummy nibh euismod tin cidunt ut laoreet dolore magna aliquam erat volutpat. Ut wisi enim ad minim veniam, quis nostrud exerci tation.

Employee-owned

Lorem ipsum dolor sit amet, consectetuer adipiscing elit, sed diam nonummy nibh euismod tin cidunt ut laoreet dolore magna aliquam erat volutpat. Ut wisi enim ad minim veniam, quis nostrud exerci tation.

Sprint. Ipsum dolor sit amet, consectetuer adipiscing elit. Sed diam nonummy nibh euismod tin cidunt ut laoreet dolore magna aliquam erat volutpat.

AT&T. Nonummy nibh euismod tin cidunt ut laoreet dolore magna aliquam erat volutpat. Ut wisi enim ad minim veniam, quis nostrud exerci tation.

Other brands. Ipsum dolor sit amet, consectetuer adipiscing elit. Sed diam nonummy nibh euismod tin cidunt ut laoreet dolore magna aliquam erat volutpat.

Pagers

At vero eros et accumsan et iusto odio dignissim qui blandit praesent luptatum zzril delenit augue feugait. Consectetuer adipiscing elit, sed diam nonummy.

Conclusion

Duis atem vel eum iriure dolor in hendrerit in vulputate velit esse molestie consequat, vel illum dolore eu feugiat nulla facilisis at vero eros et accumsan et iusto odio dignissim qui blandit praesent luptatum zzril delenit augue duis dolore te feugait nulla facilisi.

Appendix E

Sample Chapter/Report With Five Heading Levels

NOTE: *The example presented in this appendix is meant for viewing of heading levels only. The length of each section as shown here is not an indication of the length that your sections should be; these sections are abbreviated due to space limitations.*

NOTE: *If you are including a title page on your report, leave the title off the first page of the actual report.*

CHAPTER FOUR

RESULTS AND FINDINGS

Lorem ipsum dolor sit amet, consectetuer adipiscing elit, sed diam nonummy nibh euismod tin cidunt ut laoreet dolore magna aliquam erat volutpat. Ut wisi enim ad minim veniam, quis nostrud exerci tation ullamcorper suscipit lobortis nisl ut aliquip ex ea commodo consequat.

Results and Findings

Lorem ipsum dolor sit amet, consectetuer adipiscing elit, sed diam nonummy nibh euismod tin cidunt ut laoreet dolore magna aliquam erat volutpat:

1. Facilisis at vero.

2. Et iusto odio dignissim.

ABC Company

Management Response

First group. Lorem ipsum dolor sit amet, consectetuer adipiscing elit, sed diam nonummy nibh euismod tin cidunt ut laoreet dolore magna aliquam erat volutpat. Ut wisi enim ad minim veniam, quis nostrud exerci tation.

Second group. Duis atem vel eum iriure dolor in hendrerit in vulputate velit esse molestie consequat. Vel illum dolore eu feugiat nulla facilisis at vero eros et accumsan et iusto odio.

<u>Employee Response</u>

<u>First group</u>.

Lorem ipsum dolor sit amet, consectetuer adipiscing elit, sed diam nonummy nibh euismod tin cidunt ut laoreet dolore magna aliquam erat volutpat. Ut wisi enim ad minim veniam, quis nostrud

exerci tation ullamcorper suscipit lobortis nisl ut aliquip ex ea commodo consequat.

Second group. Nam liber tempor cum soluta nobis eleifend option congue nihil imperdiet doming id quod mazim placerat facer possim assum. Lorem ipsum dolor sit amet, consectetuer adipiscing elit.

XYZ Company

Management Response

First group. Lorem ipsum dolor sit amet, consectetuer adipiscing elit, sed diam nonummy nibh euismod tin cidunt ut laoreet dolore magna aliquam erat volutpat. Ut wisi enim ad minim veniam, quis nostrud exerci tation ullamcorper suscipit lobortis nisl ut aliquip ex ea commodo consequat.

Second group. Duis atem vel eum iriure dolor in hendrerit in vulputate velit esse molestie consequat, vel illum dolore eu feugiat nulla facilisis at vero eros et accumsan et iusto odio dignissim qui blandit praesent luptatum zzril delenit augue duis dolorre te feugait nulla facilisi.

Employee Response

First group. Lorem ipsum dolor sit amet, consectetuer adipiscing elit, sed diam nonummy nibh euismod tin cidunt ut laoreet dolore magna aliquam erat volutpat. Ut wisi enim ad minim veniam, quis nostrud exerci tation ullamcorper suscipit lobortis nisl ut aliquip ex ea commodo consequat.

Second group. Nam liber tempor cum soluta nobis eleifend option congue nihil imperdiet doming id quod mazim placerat facer possim assum. Lorem ipsum dolor sit amet, consectetuer adipiscing elit, sed diam nonummy nibh euismod tin cidunt ut laoreet dolore magna aliquam erat volutpat.

Analysis

Duis atem vel eum iriure dolor in hendrerit in vulputate velit esse molestie consequat, vel illum dolore eu feugiat nulla facilisis at vero eros et accumsan et iusto odio dignissim qui blandit praesent luptatum zzril delenit augue duis dolore te feugait nulla facilisi. Nam liber tempor cum soluta nobis eleifend option congue nihil imperdiet doming id quod mazim placerat facer possim assum.

Conclusion

Nam liber tempor cum soluta nobis eleifend option congue nihil imperdiet doming id quod mazim placerat facer possim assum. Lorem ipsum dolor sit amet, consectetuer adipiscing elit, sed diam nonummy nibh euismod tin cidunt ut laoreet dolore magna aliquam erat volutpat.

Appendix F

Sample Reference List

References

American Management Association (1992). *PCs today.* New York: Author.

Bernstein, T. M. (1965). *The careful writer: A modern guide to English usage.* New York: Atheneum.

Harrison, P. R. (1989). *The Manager's World* (F. G. Taylor, Ed.). Los Angeles: Business Press.

Jones, J. (Ed.). (1992). *PCs today.* New York: Doubleday.

Kendall, J. T. (1992). The modern manager. In *21st century business.* New York: Doubleday.

Lopez, T. L. (1992). The workplace in the year 2000. In S. L. Graves (Ed.), *PCs today* (pp. 201-210). New York: Acme Press.

Morrison, H. A. (1992, December). The paperless office. *Business Talk, 115,* 70-76.

Parris, C. A. (1969). *Mastering executive arts and skills.* New York: Atheneum.

RU486: The import ban and its effect on medical research: Hearings before the Subcommittee on Regulation, Business Opportunities, and Energy, of the House Committee on Small Business, 101st Cong., 35 (1990) (testimony of Ronald Chesemore).

S. 5936, 102d Cong., 2d Sess. § 4(1992).

Spetch, M. L., & Wilkie, D. M. (1983). *How to bullet-proof your manuscript*. New York: Atheneum.

The student's dictionary (4th ed.). (1992). New York: Wallace.

Williams, J. G. (2002, March). Twelve ways to motivate your employees. *Management Today*, 4(14). Retrieved from http://www.managementtoday.com/subscribe/newsletter6.html

A

B

C

R

About the Author

Carol J. Amato is a writer, editor, trainer, anthropologist, and educator. As a writer, she has published fourteen books, over 175 articles, and two short stories. She has written software user manuals, training guides, policy and procedure manuals, marketing materials, and general business documents for software development firms, banks, aerospace, and commercial industry.

Her editorial experience includes twelve books, two book series, and numerous articles, and she has served as editor for two magazines and several newsletters. She is a guest lecturer, has given many papers at conferences, and has appeared on television and radio shows.

Ms. Amato conducts communications training seminars in the corporate world and train-the-trainer seminars in the academic arena. Formerly, she conducted software training seminars in companies in the L.A.-Orange County area.

As an anthropologist, she has conducted research in the social and psychological problems associated with living in isolated and confined environments, such as undersea labs, Arctic and Antarctic research labs, space habitats, submarines, oil tankers, etc.

An adjunct faculty member of the University of Phoenix (Online and Southern California Campuses), where she teaches communications classes, Ms. Amato is the Area Chair of Communications for the Online Campus. She served as the Area Chair of Communications at the San Diego Campus from 1990-1994. In addition, she has taught at the junior high and high school levels, both in the United States and England.

Ms. Amato has a B.A. in Spanish and French from the University of Portland in Portland, Oregon, and an M.A. in Environmental Anthropology from California State University, Fullerton, California. She is a past president of the Professional Writers of Orange County and a board member of the Writer's Club of Whittier, Inc., a professional writers' workshop. She was a board member of the Orange County Section of the Independent Writers of Southern California from 1988-1993. She is listed in *Who's Who in America, Who's Who of American Women*, *Who's Who in the West*, *Who's Who in Orange County*, and the *World Who's Who of Women*.

A user-friendly tutorial for using the MLA

The World's Easiest Guide to Using the MLA is packed with all the essential information any student needs to use the Modern Language Association (MLA) style guide in a high-school or undergraduate report. It is also designed as a guide for faculty who are teaching students this particular style and is of special benefit to English-as-a-second-language students.

This user-friendly tutorial provides easy-to-follow instructions with detailed illustrations for:

- setting up pages

- placing graphics

- formatting mathematical and statistical information

- using seriation and abbreviations

- documenting sources in the text

- formatting frontis material and appendices

- creating a works cited list

- punctuation and spelling

In addition, *The World's Easiest Guide to Using the MLA* includes a sample report and works cited list.

The World's Easiest Guide to Using the MLA

A User-Friendly Manual for Formatting Research Papers According to the Modern Language Association Style Guide

Carol J. Amato

ISBN: 0-9643853-6-8 (College Edition, Paper)
ISBN: 0-9643853-7-6 (Library Edition, Spiral)
$19.95
368 pages

STARGAZER
Publishing Company
PO Box 77002
Corona, CA 92877-0100

"The World's Easiest Style Guides"

**To order, call (800) 606-7895
FAX (951) 898-4633
or order online at www.stargazerpub.com**

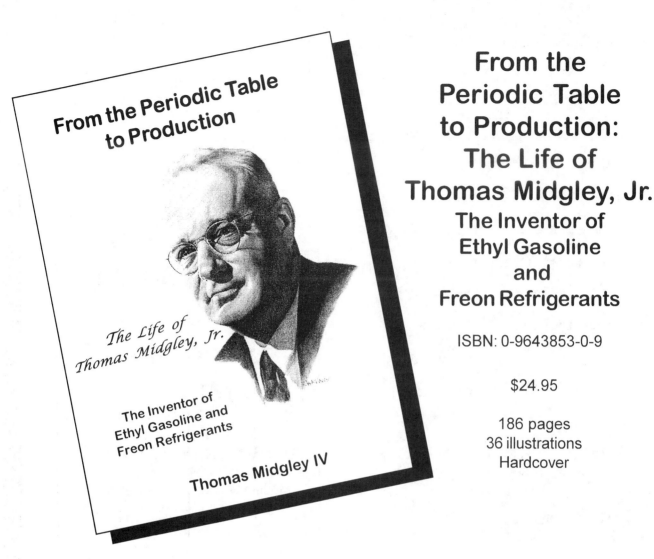

From the Periodic Table to Production: The Life of Thomas Midgley, Jr.
The Inventor of Ethyl Gasoline and Freon Refrigerants

ISBN: 0-9643853-0-9

$24.95

186 pages
36 illustrations
Hardcover

One of the noted creative men of the 20th century, Thomas Midgley discovered chemical antiknock agents, conceived a method for extracting bromine from the ocean, developed a new series of nontoxic and noninflammable refrigerating gases based on flourine, conducted extensive research on rubber, and developed the Midgley Optical Gas Engine Indicator.

How did Thomas Midgley, Jr., a mechanical engineer, make all these important advances in chemistry even after an attack of polio in 1940 made him a semi-invalid? Said Charles F. Kettering at the time of Midgley's untimely passing at the age of 54 in 1946, this "is one of the unusual stories in modern research."

From the Periodic Table to Production is the first in Stargazer's new series of biographies of people who have made significant contributions to the sciences, arts, and humanities. Written by Midgley's grandson, Thomas Midgley IV, this book chronicles the scientist's life, focusing on the twenty years during which Midgley made most of his discoveries. On May 3, 2003, Thomas Midgley, Jr., was inducted into the National Inventors' Hall of Fame in Akron, Ohio.

STARGAZER
Publishing Company

PO Box 77002
Corona, CA 92877-0100

"Educate, Enlighten, Empower"

To order, call (800) 606-7895
FAX (951) 898-4633
or order online at www.stargazerpub.com

STARGAZER
Publishing Company
PO Box 77002
Corona, CA 92877-0100

"The World's Easiest Style Guides"

Order Form

✔ Yes! Rush me the following items!

QTY.	ISBN	TITLE	PRICE	AMOUNT
_____	0-9713756-6-6	*The World's Easiest Guide to Using the APA*, 3rd edition, spiral bound	$21.95	$_____
_____	0-9713756-7-4	*The World's Easiest Guide to Using the APA*, 3rd edition, perfect bound	$21.95	$_____
_____	0-9543853-6-8	*The World's Easiest Guide to Using the MLA*, spiral bound	$19.95	$_____
_____	0-9543853-7-6	*The World's Easiest Guide to Using the MLA*, perfect bound	$19.95	$_____
_____	0-9543853-8-4	*The World's Easiest Guide to Using the MLA*, Software Referencing Program	$9.95	$_____
_____	0-9713756-0-9	*From the Periodic Table to Production: The Life of Thomas Midgley, Jr.*, hardcover	$24.95	$_____

All orders must be prepaid.   Sales tax 7.75% (CA residents only) $_____
No checks.

SUBTOTAL $_____

Shipping/handling: $3.00 per book Media Rate* $_____
$8. 50 per book Priority Mail/UPS*

Shipping cost subject to change   **TOTAL** $_____

METHOD OF PAYMENT: ❏ Amex   ❏ Visa   ❏ MasterCard   ❏ Discover

Card Number_____

Expiration Date_____ Signature_____

SHIPPING METHOD: ❏ Media Rate   ❏ Priority Mail   ❏ Other _____

SHIP TO:

Name_____

Address**_____

Address_____

City _____State_____Zip_____

Phone Number _____

**If not the same as the address on your credit card, please add billing address on the second address line.*

(800) 606-7895 • e-mail: stargazer@stargazerpub.com • **FAX (951) 898-4633**

Order online at www.stargazerpub.com

STARGAZER
Publishing Company
PO Box 77002
Corona, CA 92877-0100

STARGAZER
Publishing Company

PO Box 77002
Corona, CA 92877-0100

"The World's Easiest Style Guides"

Reader Comment Card

We have tried to make these instructions accurate, complete, and readable, yet understandable to the undergraduate. Please take a moment to tell us what you think.

How useful was *The World's Easiest Guide to Using the APA* in completing your report, project, or thesis?

❑ Excellent   ❑ Good   ❑ Average   ❑ Poor

Check what you feel are the best features of this reference guide:

_____ well-organized   _____ clearly written   _____ well-illustrated   _____ fully-researched

Should anything be added?

_____

_____

_____

_____

Should anything be deleted or corrected? Please give the page, paragraph, and line number, and a brief explanation here:

_____

_____

_____

_____

_____

What is your overall rating of this reference guide?

❑ Excellent   ❑ Good   ❑ Average   ❑ Poor

Your name _____

College name _____Phone_____

Address _____

City_____ State _____ ZIP _____

Thank you for your time!

(800) 606-7895   •   **(951)** 898-4619   •   **FAX (951) 898-4633**   •   e-mail: stargazer@stargazerpub.com

www.stargazerpub.com

STARGAZER
Publishing Company
PO Box 77002
Corona, CA 92877-0100